Biblical Worldview II
Applying a Biblical Worldview

BWVW 102

Dr. N. Troy Matthews
Liberty University

Biblical Worldview II: Applying a Biblical Worldview – BWVW 102
Copyright © 2013 by Troy Matthews, Ed.D.

Scripture taken from the Holy Bible, King James Version, New Living Translation, New International Version.

All rights reserved. No part of this publication may be reproduced or transmitted in any form or by any means, electronic or mechanical, including photocopying, recording, or any information storage and retrieval system, without the written permission of the publisher.

Requests for permission to make copies of any part of the work should be mailed to:

Permissions Department
Academx Publishing Services, Inc.
P.O. Box 208
Sagamore Beach, MA 02562

Printed in the United States of America

ISBN-10: 1-60036-552-3
ISBN-13: 978-1-60036-552-2

TABLE OF CONTENTS

CHAPTER 1:
    Biblical Worldview (Review) 1

CHAPTER 2:
    Christian/Community Service (CSER) 7

CHAPTER 3:
    Abortion 21

CHAPTER 4:
    Euthanasia 33

CHAPTER 5:
    Gender Issues 43

CHAPTER 6:
    Homosexuality 47

CHAPTER 7:
    Dating Relationships 53

CHAPTER 8:
    Marriage & Divorce 61

CHAPTER 9:
    Racial Issues 67

CHAPTER 10:
    Alcohol & Drug Abuse 73

CHAPTER 11:
    Poverty & the Poor 81

CHAPTER 12:
    Work Ethic 87

CHAPTER 13:
    Conflict Resolution 91

BIBLIOGRAPHY: 97

Chapter One

BIBLICAL WORLDVIEW

Affirming a Biblical Worldview – A Review from Semester 1

> "A world view is a set of presuppositions (assumptions which may be true, partially true or entirely false) which we hold (consciously or subconsciously, consistently or inconsistently) about the basic make-up of our world."
>
> James W. Sire *The Universe Next Door*, (Intervarsity, 1988)

I. **Five Key Questions that Define your Worldview**

1) The question of **Origin**

   Genesis 1:1 (NKJV) - *In the beginning God created the heavens and the earth.*

   Genesis 1:26-27 (NKJV) - *Then God said, "Let Us make man in Our image, according to Our likeness; let them have dominion over the fish of the sea, over the birds of the air, and over the cattle, over all the earth and over every creeping thing that creeps on the earth." So God created man in His own image; in the image of God He created him; male and female He created them.*

   "How did life begin in the first place?"
   "Where did I come from?"

2) The question of **Identity**

   Genesis 1:27-28 (NKJV) - *So God created man in His own image; in the image of God He created him; male and female He created them. Then God blessed them, and God said to them, "Be fruitful and multiply; fill the earth and subdue it; have dominion over the fish of the sea, over the birds of the air, and over every living thing that moves on the earth."*

   Romans 3:23 (NIV) - *for all have sinned and fall short of the glory of God*

   "What does it mean to be a human?"
   "Am I more important than animals?"

Chapter One – A Biblical Worldview (Review)

3) The question of __Meaning__ (purpose)

Matthew 22:37-40 (ESV) - *And he said to him, "You shall love the Lord your God with all your heart and with all your soul and with all your mind. This is the great and first commandment. And a second is like it: You shall love your neighbor as yourself. On these two commandments depend all the Law and the Prophets."*

Matthew 28:18-20 (NIV) *Then Jesus came to them and said, "All authority in heaven and on earth has been given to me. Therefore go and make disciples of all nations, baptizing them in the name of the Father and of the Son and of the Holy Spirit, and teaching them to obey everything I have commanded you. And surely I am with you always, to the very end of the age."*

"Why are we here?"
"Why am I here?"

4) The question of __Morality__ (ethics)

Matthew 22:37-40 (see verses above)

"What is meant by right and wrong?"
"How should I live?"

5) The question of __Destiny__

Hebrews 9:27-28 (ESV) - *And just as it is appointed for man to die once, and after that comes judgment…*

Philippians 1:21, 23 (NIV) - *For to me, to live is Christ and to die is gain. I am torn between the two: I desire to depart and be with Christ, which is better by far.*

Revelation 20:11-15 (NET) - *Then I saw a large white throne and the one who was seated on it; the earth and the heaven fled from his presence, and no place was found for them. And I saw the dead, the great and the small, standing before the throne. Then books were opened, and another book was opened – the book of life. So the dead were judged by what was written in the books, according to their deeds.*

"Is there life after death?"
"What will happen to me when I die?"
"Will I have to answer for how I lived my life?"

Chapter One – A Biblical Worldview (Review)

II. **The Basis of a Biblical Worldview**

A. _God exists_ – (Genesis 1:1)

B. God has revealed _Himself_ to mankind – (Hebrews 1:1-2)

C. _Jesus_ is God's son who is the redeemer of the world – (John 3:16)

D. The Bible is God's _Word_ – (II Tim. 3:16; II Peter 1:20-21)

E. Christians are to follow the teachings of the _Bible_ (II Tim. 3:16-17; I Peter 1:16)

Why is it important that we understand our worldview?

The Worldview Triangle/Pyramid

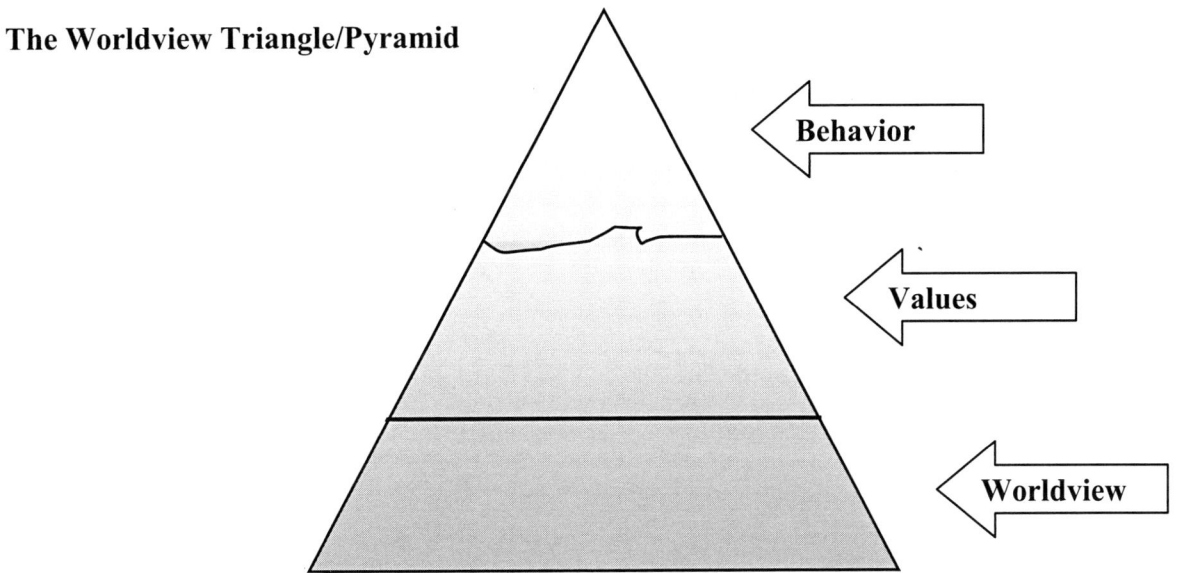

Our behavior is shaped by our values, which are ultimately built upon the foundation of our worldview

McDowell, Josh. & Bob Hostetler. *Beyond Belief to Conviction.* (Wheaton, IL; Tyndale House, 2002)

Chapter One – A Biblical Worldview (Review)

"Most discussions about Christian worldview formation correctly presuppose that students come to our colleges and universities as individuals whose minds need to be cultivated to think about their lives and chosen disciplines. However, there seems to be little emphasis on the fact that our students come to us possessing a variety of worldviews already. Their worldviews are the products of countless agents acting on them – peers, their culture, their particular denominational heritage, their own spiritual journey, their education to date…. Thus when we endeavor to communicate a Christian worldview, we are not starting with open plots ready for cultivation; we are starting with densely populated intellectual ground with various worldviews firmly entrenched and others competing for space.

(Kanitz, Lori. *Improving Christian Worldview Pedagogy: Going Beyond Mere Christianity.* Christian Higher Education, Taylor Francis Inc. 2005)

The values of thinking through (cultivating) your worldview.
(Or why be concerned about worldview?)

- Helps you to clarify the important issues and ideas of life.
- Helps you see how the "bits and pieces" fit into the "bigger picture."
- Helps you appreciate the "beauty" of the Christian worldview as a coherent, adequate and relevant system of thought.
- Helps you identify and resist non- and anti-Christian "winds of doctrine." (Ephesians 4:14)
- Helps you to logically make a case for your beliefs to others. (1 Peter 3:15)
- Helps you to intelligently challenge others to explain and defend their belief systems (both Christians and non-Christians – everyone has to do apologetics!)
- Prepares you to give the answers to the questions people are really concerned about. (Who am I? Why am I here? Where did all this come from? Why do we suffer? How can I know there's a God? Etc.)
- Equips you to engage your culture more intelligently and effectively as you focus on the root causes of the "issues" rather than just the issues themselves.

Worldview Review
(Comparative Chart of Naturalism and Biblical Theism)

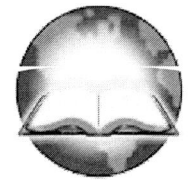

Important Note: These are obviously not the definite outcomes of either one of these worldviews. That is, the naturalist or secularist will not hold to all the viewpoints on the left column. And some who claim biblical theism will not consistently hold to every point in the right column. Both theists and non-theists inconsistently "borrow" from the other's worldview, often without realizing it, and usually for convenience sake. What these represent are the logical consequences of these primary belief systems. As biblical theists, we should seek to be more and more consistent with the right column when we think about and do ethics. And we must be able to show the naturalist/secularist the logical outcomes of his or her starting point.

Naturalism (Humanism, Secularism, Postmodernism)	Biblical Theism
God <u>DOES NOT</u> exist (Humanism/Materialism) or God's existence is <u>IRRELEVANT</u> to human life (Secularism).	A <u>PERSONAL</u> God exists as Creator, Sustainer, and Ruler of all. (Exodus 20:11, Nehemiah 9:6, Psalm 33:6)
<u>ANTHROPO</u>centric	<u>THEO</u>centric (1 Corinthians 10:31)
Humans are <u>ACCIDENTAL</u> products of chance <u>EVOLUTION</u> with no ultimate <u>PURPOSE</u> for being	Humans are <u>SPECIAL</u> creations <u>DESIGNED</u> by God to glorify Him and reflect His nature (Genesis 1:26-27, 2:7, Revelation 4:11)
Human life has <u>EXTRINSIC (CONDITIONAL)</u> value	Human life has <u>INTRINSIC (UNCONDITIONAL)</u> value (Genesis 1:27, 9:6, Psalm 8:4-5, Mark 8:36-37, James 3:9)
<u>QUALITY</u> of life	<u>SANCTITY</u> of life (Isaiah 46:3-4)
Man is <u>A SELF DETERMINED SOVEREIGN</u>	Man is <u>A SUBMISSIVE STEWARD</u> (Genesis 1:28 2:15, Psalm 8:6-8)
Human <u>AUTONOMY</u>	Divine <u>AUTHORITY</u> (Genesis 2:16-17, Isaiah 33:22)
Moral knowledge through unaided human <u>REASON</u>	Moral knowledge through divine <u>REVELATION</u> and reason (Proverbs 20:27, Romans 2:14,15, 2 Timothy 3:16,)

Chapter One – A Biblical Worldview (Review)

Naturalism (Humanism, Secularism, Postmodernism)	Biblical Theism
All moral truth originates in and is **DEPENDENT** upon human experience (**REALTIVE/SUBJECTIVE**)	Some moral truth is **OUTSIDE OF** and **INDEPENDENT** from human experience (**ABSOLUTE/OBJECTIVE**)
Ethical Emphasis: **TELEOLOGICAL** *"The ends JUSTIFY the means"*	Ethical Emphasis: **DEONTOLOGICAL** *"The ends and means must be JUST"*
Man **CONTROLS** and **MANIPULATES** nature according to **HUMAN WISH**.	Man **COOPERATES** with and **MAINTAINS** creation according to **DIVINE WILL** ("Cultural Mandate" Genesis 1:26-28)
TECHNOLOGY (ability) determines **MORALITY**	**MORALITY** limits **TECHNOLOGY** (can does not equal should)
SUFFERING is senseless	Suffering has **VALUE** (Romans 5:3-4, James 1:2-4)
Right to **DIE**	Responsibility to respect **LIFE** (including my own) (Exodus 20:13, Romans 13:8-10)
Death **ENDS** all **SUFFERING**	Death may begin **ENDLESS SUFFERING** (Revelation 20:11-15)
At death: **NO ACCOUNTABILITY** for what we believed and how we behaved.	At death: **ACCOUNTABILITY** for what we believed and how we behaved (Ecclesiastes 11:9, 12:14, Matthew 12:36, Hebrews 9:27)

"I believe in Christianity like I believe that the sun has risen, not only because I can see it, but by it I see everything else."
C.S Lewis – *The Weight of Glory*

Chart Prepared by:
Dr. W.E. Honeycutt - Assistant Professor of Contemporary Issues (Liberty University)

Chapter One – A Biblical Worldview (Review)

Chapter Two

CHRISTIAN/COMMUNITY SERVICE (CSER)

The Center for Christian/Community Service

Liberty University Christian/Community Service (CSER) Official Policy Handbook

The following information needs to be read and understood by both Liberty students and supervisors who work with Liberty students. Any questions or concerns not covered by the following policies should be directed to the Center for CSER.

Location: Green Hall room 1880
Hours: M-F 8:00 a.m. – 4:30 p.m.
Phone: (434) 582-2325
FAX: (434) 582-2660
E-mail: cser@liberty.edu

Our Mission

In recognition of the scriptural admonition that "faith without works is dead" (James 2:17) and in fulfillment of the Great Commission of world evangelization found in Matt. 28:18-20, the Christian/Community Service component of the curriculum serves to affirm the Christian worldview and provide a practical expression of God's love for mankind.

Our Purpose

The Center for Christian/Community Service seeks to support the University in fulfilling its Mission and Aims by providing experiences for students that:

1. Promote the development of the Christian worldview as it impacts upon lifestyles, decision making, personal integrity, and social responsibility.
2. Develop a sense of responsibility to mankind which entails selfless service, and active and clear communication of the Christian faith.
3. Offer opportunities for students to explore and practice ways in which they may glorify God and advance the cause of Christ through their chosen careers.

 **THINKING**

"We at Liberty University require Christian/Community Service so that our young people get an action-oriented curriculum. When you go to a Christian university you need not only to learn the information in the class room, but you need to take it out to the people; out to the neighborhoods and the communities; the hospitals and homes. Christian Service for us is a part of the Liberty curriculum; a part of the action-oriented curriculum and it shall ever be a part of Liberty."

Jerry Falwell, Chancellor of Liberty University
May 1, 2002

Chapter Two - CSER

THINKING

"The mission here has always been to train young Champions for Christ whose main calling is to serve Christ and their fellow man. The core of Christianity is to love the Lord your God with all your heart, soul and mind, and to love your neighbor as yourself. So that's what we try to teach through the Christian/Community Service program here at Liberty; to love your neighbor by serving your neighbor. It's so important for these students to learn to give back and serve others like Jesus did. Jesus was a servant leader, and what we try to teach through this program is servant leadership."

Jerry Falwell Jr.
Chancellor, Liberty University
April 29, 2009

4. Provide avenues to explore ways of displaying Christian commitment and virtue through local churches, or social, civic, athletic, artistic, and scholastic organizations which are compatible with the University's overall mission

To fulfill Christian/Community Service (CSER) graduation requirements, students and supervisors must understand particular aspects about four areas:

I) Criteria,
II) Enrollment,
III) Participation
IV) Evaluation & Credit.

The following policies are arranged in an FAQ format to facilitate understanding.

Academic Designation numbers for CSER

- 100's - BWVW - Biblical Worldview I & II
- 200's – Church ministries
- 300's – Campus service opportunities
- 400's – Athletics (Team organized service)
- 500's – Community organizations

Christian/Community Services (CSERs) are categorized as follows. The numbering system in CSER does not represent student ranking. <u>Once a student has completed BWVW 101 and 102, he or she is free to choose from any of the 200s, 300s, 400s, or 500s.</u> (The actual registration process is described below in Section II E.)

(Note: There are prerequisites for some opportunities, but these are imposed by the supervisors, not the Center for CSER or Liberty University).

Chapter Two - CSER

Section I - Criteria

A. What qualifies as a valid CSER?
1. To receive CSER credit students may not:
   a. Receive monetary compensation
   b. Receive academic credit
   c. Be awarded a scholarship

2. A CSER must fit within the framework of the missions and goals of the department, which may include any, or all, of the following:
   a. Evangelism
   b. Discipleship
   c. Tutoring/mentoring
   d. Civic and community services (this does not include political campaigning)
   e. Community improvement
   f. Alleviation of human suffering
   g. Assisting the underprivileged and less fortunate
   h. Education and development of children/adults
   i. Educational assistance
   j. Stewardship of the earth (Environmental projects, care for animals, etc.)

See our listing of CSER opportunities that fit these criteria.

B. Can a CSER be fulfilled with an organization other than is listed?
Yes. This falls under the areas of Special Projects (399s) and Church Extensions (279s) and requires special application. In these cases, there must be strict adherence to the following:

1. Special Projects (399s)
   a. Students are expected to respect the doctrinal and ethical positions of Liberty University.
   b. Students must submit an application online through ASIST and receive approval through the Center for CSER prior to receiving credit. Students will need the name and email address of the person who will be supervising and evaluating their service before applying online

2. Church Extensions (279s)
   a. Students are expected to respect the doctrinal and ethical positions of Liberty University.
   b. Students must submit an application online through ASIST and receive approval through the Center for CSER prior to receiving credit. Students will need the name and email address of the person who will be supervising and evaluating their service before applying online.
   c. The Center for CSER requires a doctrinal statement from a prospective church. The church will be evaluated in light of the University's doctrinal statement.

Note: Without prior approval from the Center for CSER for 279s and 399s, students run the risk of having their CSERs denied due to their failure to conform to established CSER criteria.

C. Can a CSER be done with a for-profit business or organization?
While the general rule is that CSERs must be done through existing non-profit 501(c)(3) organizations, it is possible that some for-profit organizations, particularly those dealing with human health and services (hospitals, nursing homes, etc.), may be approved as CSER sites. Further, if a business is involved in a not-for-profit community service endeavor, this may be considered a valid CSER opportunity provided the minimal 20 hours (See Section III.C.) can be completed. Strict guidelines must be followed in these situations. Requests for exceptions will be dealt with on a case by case basis. It is mandatory that students make application and receive approval through the Center for CSER prior to receiving credit.

Note: Without prior approval from the Center for CSER, students run the risk of having their CSERs denied due to their failure to conform to established CSER criteria.

D. May students use their internship at a non-profit organization for a CSER?
While you may not receive CSER credit for the work for which you are being paid or are receiving academic credit (Section I.A.1), you may do additional hours for CSER credit. Each situation will be handled on a case by case basis.

Note: Internships at for-profit organizations may not be used for CSER credit.

E. Can students fulfill their CSERs by volunteering at someone's home?
No. Any exceptions to this policy require Center for CSER approval.

Note: Without prior approval from the Center for CSER, students run the risk of having their CSERs denied due to their failure to conform to established CSER criteria.

Section II: Enrollment

A. Who must enroll in CSER?
1. All residential undergraduate students who are full-time during the fall or spring semester are required to be enrolled in a CSER. Undergraduate students are considered full-time if they are taking twelve (12) or more credit hours in a given semester.
2. According to the student's Degree Completion Plan (DCP), BWVW 101 and BWVW 102 are a student's first two CSER requirements.

B. What are BWVW 101 and BWVW 102?

According to the student's Degree Completion Plan (DCP), BWVW 101 and BWVW 102 are a student's first two CSER requirements.

1. BWVW 101: BIBLICAL WORLDVIEW I

    This course is designed to aid the student in the development of a biblical worldview. This will involve an introduction to critical thinking, an evaluation of contemporary moral philosophies, and an affirmation of absolute truth. Students will be challenged to integrate a biblical worldview into their Christian/Community Service.
    BWVW 101 is a prerequisite for BWVW 102

2. BWVW 102: BIBLICAL WORLDVIEW II

    This course is a study of contemporary moral issues encountered by students in their Christian/Community Service. Students will be challenged to evaluate these issues and understand their responsibilities to them in light of a biblical worldview.
    *Prerequisite: **BWVW 101***

Note: Students who have failed either or both BWVWs will be required to enroll in the needed CSERs to keep from falling behind in their graduation requirements. These students will be doing CSER while simultaneously completing their BWVW requirements.

C. When may a student enroll in a CSER?

Students may enroll during the fall, spring or summer semesters.

Note: Although CSER is not required during the summer semester, a CSER earned over the summer may count for a previous or future semester (See details at Section IV.G. below)

1. **FALL SEMESTER** - The Christian/Community Service Registration Fair occurs during the first week of the fall semester. CSER supervisors are invited to represent their area of service and register students. Students are not required to register during the fair, but are encouraged to do so. Otherwise, they are responsible to submit an application online through ASIST before the Add/Drop deadline. **Students will need the name and email address of the person who will be supervising and evaluating their service before applying online.**

    The Drop/Add deadline for the FALL semester is the first Monday in October. A $10.00 late fee will be added to the student's Liberty University account after this date.

    <u>ALL HOURS MUST BE COMPLETED WITHIN THE FALL SEMESTER.</u>
    Note: CSERs REGISTERED FOR IN THE FALL WILL AUTOMATICALLY CARRY OVER TO THE SPRING SEMESTER, BUT NOT THE SUMMER

SEMESTER. Students must understand that they are making **a one-year commitment** to the organization when they enroll in the fall semester. If they wish to change CSERs in the spring, they must follow the proper procedures (See Section II.E. below).

2. **SPRING SEMESTER** – There is no Registration Fair in the spring semester. Consequently, students enrolling in CSER for the spring semester are responsible to submit an application online through ASIST by the Add/Drop deadline. **Students will need the name and email address of the person who will be supervising and evaluating their service before applying online**

   The Drop/Add deadline for the SPRING semester is the first Monday in March. A $10.00 late fee will be added to the student's Liberty University account after this date.

   ALL HOURS MUST BE COMPLETED WITHIN THE SPRING SEMESTER.

3. **SUMMER SEMESTER** - Students must submit an application online through ASIST by the Add/Drop deadline. **Students will need the name and email address of the person who will be supervising and evaluating their service before applying online.** A CSER earned during the summer semester can count for any semester needed for graduation. Students may also complete a CSER during the summer if they are behind in the CSER requirements (See Section III.F.).

   The Drop/Add deadline for the SUMMER semester is the first Monday in July. A $10.00 late fee will be added to the student's Liberty University account after this date.

   ALL HOURS MUST BE COMPLETED WITHIN THE SUMMER SEMESTER.

4. **WINTER BREAK** - Students must submit an application online through ASIST by the Add/Drop deadline. **Students will need the name and email address of the person who will be supervising and evaluating their service before applying online.** A CSER earned during the Winter Break can count for any semester needed for graduation. Students may also complete a CSER during the Winter Break if they are behind in the CSER requirements (See Section III.F.).

   The Add/Drop deadline for Winter Break is the first Monday in January. A $10.00 late fee will be added to the student's Liberty University account after this date.

   ALL HOURS MUST BE COMPLETED WITHIN THE WINTER BREAK.

D. Do students need to <u>re-register</u> their fall CSERs in the spring semester?

No. CSERs REGISTERED FOR IN THE FALL WILL AUTOMATICALLY CARRY OVER TO THE SPRING SEMESTER, BUT NOT THE SUMMER SEMESTER. Students must understand that they are making a <u>one-year commitment</u> to the organization when they enroll in the fall semester.

E. May students Change, Drop or Add CSERs?

Yes. Students wishing to <u>change, add or drop</u> a CSER must obtain signed permission from their CSER supervisor and receive approval from the Center for CSER. The drop add process is completed online through the following process.

ONLINE: CSER <u>(ADD)</u> Registration Process

In order to register a CSER follow these steps:
1. Log into ASIST
2. Click on "Student"
3. Click on "Registration"
4. Click on "Christian Service"
5. Click on "CSER Registration for Residential Students"
6. Log into the portal with your Liberty username and password.
7. Select the semester for which you need to register.
8. From the drop down menu select your CSER number.
9. If you are doing a CSER 279 or 399, the next drop down list is organized by state. Select your organization form the list. If it is not listed, select "Not Listed"
10. If your CSER is not listed enter information into the requested fields. (Please note that you will need to have the Supervisors NAME and E-MAIL address to complete this step)
11. E-sign and submit CSER application.

When you submit your application you will receive a confirmation code and e-mail. Your supervisor will also receive an e-mail within 24 hours letting him/her know that you have requested for them to take the next step in processing your registration.

Note: *A $10.00 late fee will be applied to every drop and every add after the deadline of a given semester.* (See Drop/Add Deadlines in Section II.C.1-4 above.).

Chapter Two - CSER

ONLINE: CSER (DROP) Process

In order to drop a previously registered CSER follow these steps:
1. Log into ASIST
2. Click on "Student"
3. Click on "Registration"
4. Click on "Christian Service"
5. Click on "CSER Registration for Residential Students"
6. Log into the portal with your Liberty username and password.
7. Select the semester for which you need to register.
8. In the semester that you selected, locate the CSER that you are wanting to "Drop"
9. On the right you will see an "Action" pull-down menu. Select "drop"
10. E-sign and submit the CSER drop form.

When you submit your CSER "drop" form you will receive a confirmation code and e-mail (KEEP A COPY OF THE CONFIRMATION NUMBER). Your supervisor will also receive an e-mail within 24 hours letting him/her know that you have requested for them to take the next step in dropping your registered CSER.

Note: *A $10.00 late fee will be applied to every drop and every add after the deadline of a given semester.* (See Drop/Add Deadlines in Section II.C.1-4 above.).

Section III: Participation

A. How many CSERs must students complete?

To graduate from Liberty, all full-time, residential undergraduate students must successfully complete one CSER requirement for each full-time semester that they are a student, up to eight (8) semesters. Undergraduate students must first pass BWVW 101 and 102 which are their first two (2) semesters of CSER requirements (See II.B.). They must then successfully complete at least one CSER for each full-time semester that they are enrolled, up to six (6) more semesters. Once students have fulfilled these requirements, they will no longer need to enroll in a CSER.

Note: Residential students who are full-time (12 hours or more) are required to enroll in CSER whether they are taking residential or LU Online courses.

B. How many CSERs may students do during a semester?

While students are only *required* to complete one CSER for every semester they are full-time, they may register and receive a grade for more than one CSER during any

Chapter Two - CSER

semester. Students who fall behind and need to receive credit for more than one CSER in a semester to fulfill their graduation requirements, must get permission from the Center for CSER (See III.F below).

C. How much time will a CSER require?
Students must complete a ***minimum*** of 20 hours in order to pass any CSER. Some supervisors may require more than 20 hours. In such cases, supervisors will inform students prior to enrollment, and then the student must complete the additional hours to pass his or her CSER with that organization. (Examples: Young Life and the local hospitals; LGH and VBH).

D. May students complete their CSER requirement during multiple semesters?
No. Students must complete all CSER hours for a registered CSER within that semester only. Semester beginning and ending dates are according to the <u>official calendar issued be the Registrar's office.</u> Summer semester and Winter Break hours must be completed between the spring and fall and fall and spring semesters respectively.

E. May students complete their CSER requirement through multiple organizations or supervisors?
No. In order to receive credit toward the fulfillment of each CSER requirement students will complete their registered CSER with one organization only and every registered CSER must be completed under one CSER supervisor only.

F. What if students fall behind in CSER?
Students may make up their CSER requirements in later semesters by completing more than one CSER in a semester. They may use the Summer semester or Winter Break to catch up as well (See Note in Section II.C. above).
1. Students may register for more than one CSER to catch up.
2. When a student registers for a CSER they can sign up for a "double registration". This would then require a minimum of 40 hours of service. (Doubling up is the maximum allowed per CSER).
3. To sign up for a "double" CSER you should ensure that you are in fact behind and then read the instruction in *red* (on the online registration form) carefully.

IT IS MANDATORY THAT STUDENTS APPLY FOR APPROVAL THROUGH THE CENTER FOR CSER BEFORE CREDIT WILL BE GIVEN FOR ANY MORE THAN ONE CSER PER SEMESTER

Chapter Two - CSER

G. What if a student receives an "F" for CSER?

The grade of "F" will remain on the student's transcript for that CSER and will not count toward fulfilling the graduation requirement unless the grade is changed through one of three ways:

1. **The Repeat Policy:** Students wishing to change a failing grade must repeat and Pass *that same CSER* under the CSER repeat policy. It is mandatory that students apply for the repeat policy through the Center for CSER before credit will be given.
2. **Drop/Add:** The drop/add process in described above in Section II E. Supervisors have full authority to deny dropping the students' CSER and in that case the Center for CSER may not change the "F." The student may then use the Repeat Policy.
3. **Missing Service Evaluation Form:** Students may have simply failed to complete the online evaluation. To correct this follow steps 1-3 of the registration process and then select Evaluation and complete the process (See Section II E.).

Section IV: Evaluation and Credit

A. What is the CSER evaluation process?

This process is central to the CSER program. When the student fulfills their hours for a registered CSER they must complete the CSER Evaluation online. Students are responsible to make sure that their exact dates and hours have been logged, that they have completed the student reflection and submitted it to their supervisor to receive their final evaluation, grade and supervisor's signature. The deadline to complete this process is posted on the CSER calendar and will be announced via a university-wide e-mail and a Splash page notification within a week of the time it is due at the end of the semester).

B. How will students be graded for their CSER?

Each student will receive a letter grade of A, B, C, D or F, according to the following criteria:

A - student displays exceptional service; excellent attitude; volunteered at least 20 hours

B - displays satisfactory service; punctuality; appropriate attitude; volunteered at least 20 hours

C - displays acceptable service; usually punctual; acceptable attitude; volunteered at least 20 hours

D - displays unsatisfactory service; not punctual; volunteered at least 20 hours

F - designates "failure"; unacceptable service; volunteered less than 20 hours

Note: Supervisors will also be required to validate each student's hours, and write out a brief personal evaluation of each student. No incomplete evaluations will be approved. An error message will be received until it is completed properly. Once the

Supervisor completes the evaluation and submits the online form the student will receive an email to complete the process so that their final grade will be posted. (This deadline date is posted on the CSER calendar and will be announced on the Splash page) within a week of the time it is due at the end of the semester).

ONLINE: CSER Evaluation Process/Form Completion

In order to complete the CSER Evaluation Process follow these steps:
1. Log into ASIST
2. Click on "Student"
3. Click on "Registration"
4. Click on "Christian Service"
5. Click on "CSER Evaluation Form for Residential Students"
6. Log into the portal with your Liberty username and password.
7. The Evaluation Form will appear.
8. Fill in the requested information.
    a. Student ID, Last Name, First Name, Email, Phone
    b. Verify the semester, Course, Organization, Supervisor
    c. Complete the Log Sheet (follow the proper date format)
    d. Select appropriate answer under Student Reflection, fill in boxes
    e. Select skill(s)
9. If you have not completed your 20 hours of CSER select SAVE and you can return to the form at a later date
10. If you have completed your 20 hours of CSER click SUBMIT and send to the CSER supervisor for evaluation.
11. After CSER supervisor completes the evaluation, the Form is ready to be signed by the student through ASIST by repeating steps 1 through 7.
12. E-sign and submit CSER Evaluation Form.

C. How may students inquire about their CSER status?
   Students who have questions or concerns regarding their CSER history and status should direct them to the Center for CSER.
   Location and Hours: Green Hall (GH) 1880, M-F 8:00 a.m. – 4:30 p.m.
   Phone: (434) 582-2325
   E-mail: cser@liberty.edu

Chapter Two - CSER

D. What should students do if there is a question or conflict concerning their registered CSER?

All questions regarding schedules, accountability procedures, grades or conflicts of any nature concerning a student's specific CSER should be initially directed to the student's supervisor for that CSER. If a satisfactory solution does not result from this meeting, the student should then contact the Center for CSER for further assistance.

E. May students receive credit for a CSER done in a previous semester for which they did not register?

Yes. However, it must meet all previously established criteria (See Section I.A). Further, the student must complete the appropriate paperwork and receive permission from the Center for CSER. By not getting prior approval the student runs the risk of having their request for credit denied due to their not meeting the established criteria. **A $10.00 late registration fee will be added to the student's Liberty University account for each CSER.**

F. May students complete extra CSERs in the fall or spring semester to count for a future semester?

No. <u>The only time in which a CSER can be completed for a future semester is during the summer and winter breaks. Only one CSER can be completed during the summer or winter to count for a future semester.</u> (See next question for how summer credits will be applied). Additional CSERs done while the student is taking BWVW will not count toward future requirements either, unless the student has failed either or both BWVWs (See section II.B. above).

G. How will CSERs completed during the summer semester be applied?

Summer and winter CSERs may be used for a previous or future semester; however, only *one* CSER per summer semester or winter break may be applied toward a future semester.

H. How will grades received for CSER affect students' GPAs?

Grades received in BWVW 101 and BWVW 102 will become a permanent part of students GPAs. Grades received for CSER will not affect their GPA, however, they will be recorded as a standard letter grade and become a permanent part of the student's school transcript.

For the most accurate and up-to-date information you should always check the CSER website or contact the office personal directly.

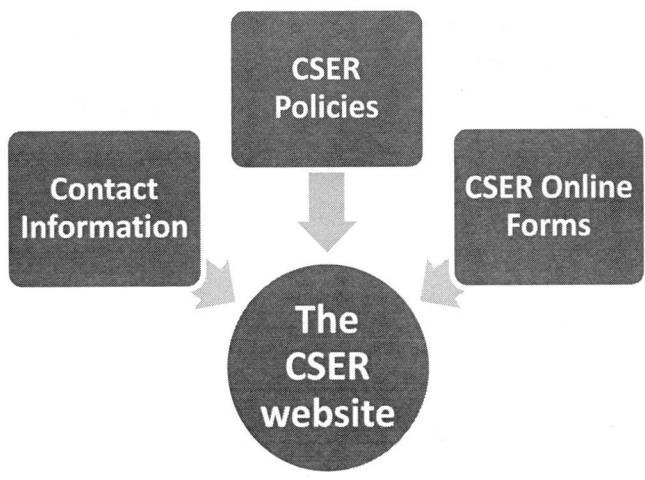

http://www.liberty.edu/CSER

Mailing Address

The Center for Christian/Community Service

Liberty University

1971 University Blvd

　Lynchburg, VA, 24502-2269

Phone: (434) 582.2325

Fax: (434) 582-2660

E-mail: CSER@liberty.edu

Campus Location: Green Hall - Room 1880

Office Hours: Mon - Fri 8:30AM - 4:30PM

Faculty and Staff:

Dr. Lew A. Weider, Director

Dr. N. Troy Matthews, Associate Director

Dr. Will Honeycutt, Assistant Director

Dr. Steve Putney, Assistant Director

Dr. Rob Van Engen, Assistant Director

Mr. Darren Wu, CSER Coordinator

Mrs. Bethany Henry, Assistant Director of Operations

Mrs. Kathy Chambers, Administrative Assistant

Chapter Two - CSER

Chapter Three

ABORTION
Applying a Biblical Worldview

Psalm 139:13,15 (KJV) - *For you formed my inward parts, you covered me in my mother's womb. My frame was not hidden from you when I was made in secret, and skillfully wrought in the lowest parts of the earth."*

Jeremiah 1:5 (NIV) – *Before I formed I formed you in the womb I knew you, before you were born I set you apart; I appointed you as a prophet to the nations.*

I. An Overview of Abortion in the United States
Developed by Physicians for Reproductive Choice and Health® (PRCH) and The Alan Guttmacher Institute (AGI)

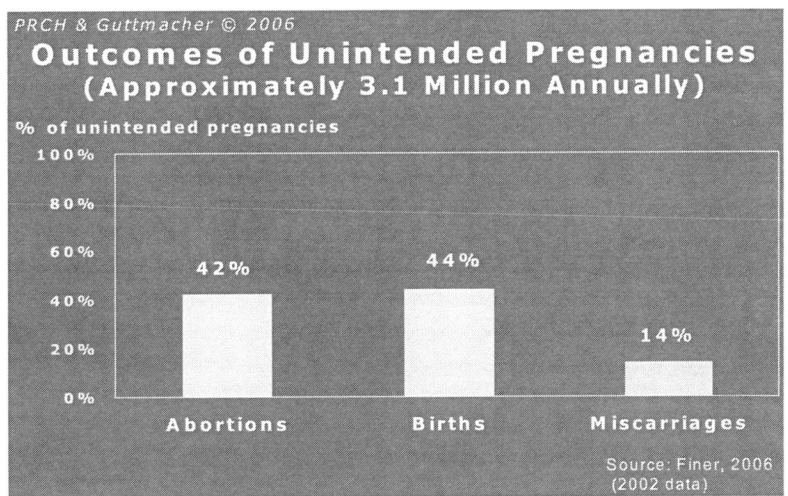

- Each year, about 1.3 million pregnancies are terminated by abortion in the United States.
- Some 2.2% of all women aged 15–44 had an abortion in 1997.
- Abortion is one of the most common surgical procedures in the United States.
- By age 20, 1 in 7 women have had at least one abortion; by age 45, 4 in 10 have done so.

DEFINITION

Abortion: the termination of a pregnancy after, accompanied by, resulting in, or closely followed by the death of the embryo or fetus:
http://www.merriam-webster.com/dictionary/abortion

Chapter Three - Abortion

Annual Number of Abortions Per 1,000 Women Aged 15–44

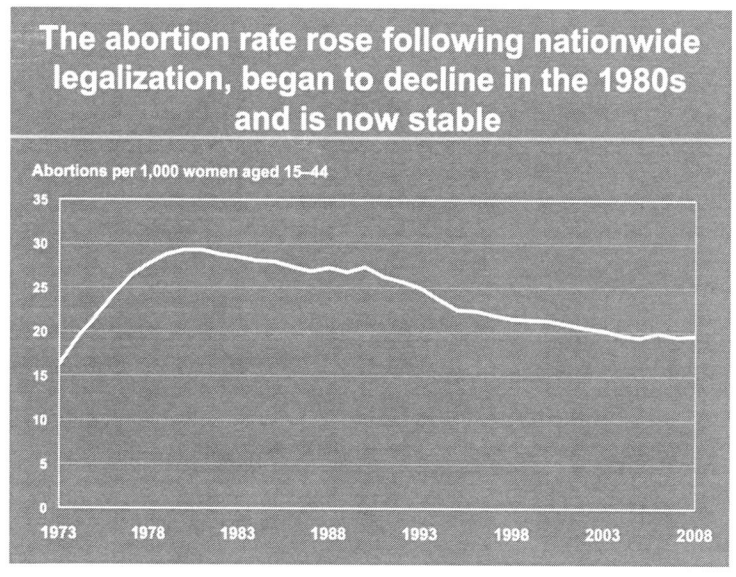

(Guttmacher Institute, 2008)

Numbers and Rates:
Global and regional estimates of induced abortion, 1995, 2003 and 2008

Region	No. of abortions (millions)			Abortion rate*		
	1995	2003	2008	1995	2003	2008
World	45.6	41.6	43.8	35	29	28
Developed countries	10.0	6.6	6.0	39	25	24
Excluding Eastern Europe	3.8	3.5	3.2	20	19	17
Developing countries	35.5	35.0	37.8	34	29	29
Excluding China	24.9	26.4	28.6	33	30	29
Africa	5.0	5.6	6.4	33	29	29
Asia	26.8	25.9	27.3	33	29	28
Europe	7.7	4.3	4.2	48	28	27
Latin America	4.2	4.1	4.4	37	31	32
North America	1.5	1.5	1.4	22	21	19
Oceania	0.1	0.1	0.1	21	18	17

*Abortions per 1,000 women aged 15–44.
Source: Sedgh G et al., Induced abortion: incidence and trends worldwide from 1995 to 2008, Lancet, 2012 (forthcoming).

GUTTMACHER INSTITUTE

THINKING

Question: Why do you think the abortion rate (while still too high) has actually decreased over the last few years?
List suggested reasons:
1.
2.
3.
4.

Question: There are groups, some have even protested at Liberty, that stand on corners holding large pictures of aborted unborn children. Do you think this is an ethical or legitimate thing to do? How effective do you think it is?
Why of why not?

Chapter Three - Abortion

Most Important Reason Given for Terminating an Unwanted Pregnancy

1. _Inadequate Finances_ 21%
2. Not ready for _responsibility_ 21%
3. Woman's life would be changed too much.................. 16%
4. Problems with _relationship_, _unmarried_ 12%
5. _Too Young_; not mature enough 11%
6. _Children all grown / no more_ 8%
7. Fetus has possible health problem 3%
8. Woman has health problem 3%
9. Pregnancy caused by _rape_ or _incest_ 1%
10. Other 4%
11. Average number of reasons given................................ 3%

Source: Torres and Forrest - AGI 2004

Commonly Used Terms:

Gamete : reproductive cell (sperm/ovum)

Zygote : formed by the union of male and female gametes (fertilization)

Embryo : the unborn from fertilization up to 3 months

Fetus : 3 months to birth.

II. Abortion: A Brief Legal History in the United States.

A. Prior to Roe V. Wade, most states made abortion a crime except for saving the mother.

B. Key Legal Cases impacting the Abortion Issue in the United States.

NOTE: An important issue on which much of the argumentation is based is the "right to privacy". This will be highlighted in class lecture.

1. _Griswold_ v. _Connecticut_ - Decided June 7, 1965

Main Ruling -

Chapter Three - Abortion

2. <u>Eisenstadt</u> v. <u>Baird</u> - Decided March 22, 1972

Main Ruling -

3. <u>Roe</u> v <u>Wade</u> - Jan. 22, 1973

Situation: Jane Roe (Norma McCorvey) –

Main Ruling - Lifted bans on abortion in all 50 states A woman's "right to privacy" extends to her liberty to terminate an unwanted pregnancy.

What the Supreme Court declared: The unborn are not "persons" and thus ineligible for constitutional protection.

- "The Constitution does not define 'person'…"
- "person" has "application only postnatally"
- "The word 'person' as used in the Fourteenth Amendment, does not include the unborn."

BIOGRAPHY

In 1970, Norma McCorvey was a young, pregnant woman in Texas without the means or funds to access an abortion. She became the plaintiff "Jane Roe" in *Roe v. Wade*, decided in 1973, one of the most famous Supreme Court decisions of the 20th century.

Norma McCorvey's identity was hidden for another decade but, during the 1980s, the public learned about the plaintiff whose lawsuit struck down most abortion laws in the United States. In 1995, Norma McCorvey made news again when she declared she had changed to a "pro-life" stance, with newfound Christian beliefs.

http://womenshistory.about.com/od/abortionus/a/norma_mccorvey.htm

The unborn are essentially non-persons

and do not fall under the protection of the 4th or 14th Amendments.

<u>IV Amendment to the U.S. Constitution</u>   "The right of the people to be secure in their persons, houses, papers, and effects, against unreasonable searches and seizures, shall not be violated, …"

<u>Amendment XIV Section 1 to the U.S. Constitution</u>   All persons born or naturalized in the United States, and subject to the jurisdiction thereof, are citizens of the United States… nor shall any State deprive any person of life, liberty, or property, without due process of law; nor deny to any person within its jurisdiction the equal protection of the laws.

Chapter Three - Abortion

4. __Doe__ v __Bolton__ - Jan. 22, 1973

Main Ruling - Expanded definition of "health" of the mother to include familial, financial, psychological, well-being, etc. as determined by her physician.

5. __Planned Parenthood__ v __Casey__ - 1992

Main ruling - Discarded 3 trimester of Roe and focused on the "viability" of the fetus as the determining point where a state's interest in unborn life begins.

6. __Partial Birth Abortion Ban Act__ - 2003

WASHINGTON, D.C. -- President Bush signed the Partial-Birth Abortion Ban Act (S. 3) into law on November 5, 2003, The bill represents the first direct national restriction on any method of abortion since the Supreme Court legalized abortion on demand in 1973.

April 18th, 2007 – A 5-4 ruling by the Supreme Court said the Partial Birth Abortion Ban Act that Congress passed and President Bush signed into law in 2003 does not violate a woman's constitutional right to an abortion.

L.E.R

III. Types of Abortion

    A. Saline Injection.

- <u>Amniotic fluid</u> is removed and replaced with a toxic saline solution
- Baby ingest the toxins and dies 1-2 hours later from salt poisoning, dehydration, and hemorrhaging
- 24 hours later the mother goes into labor delivering a dead baby
- Chemical burning of the skin causes a painful death for the baby

    B. Hysteronomy.

- Used in last trimester
- Baby removed as in a Cesarean birth
- Baby set aside and allowed to die or killed by a deliberate act

    C. Suction & Aspiration.

- Used on 80% of abortions up to 12th week of pregnancy

- Mouth of the cervix is dilated
- Hollow tube with knifelike edged tip is inserted into the womb
- A suction machine with force 28 times greater than a vacuum cleaner literally rips the developing baby to pieces and sucks the remains into a container to be disposed

D. Dilation and Curettage.

- Dilate cervix to allow the insertion of curetta—a loop-shaped knife—into the womb
- Instrument scrapes placenta from the uterus and cuts baby apart; pieces are drawn through the cervix
- Baby is re-assembled to be sure that all parts are accounted for
- If parts are left inside, the mother could bleed or become infected

E. Dilation and Evacuation.

- Used between 12 and 24 weeks
- The child is cut to pieces by a sharp knife, as in D & C
- The child is much larger and far more developed
- The child weighs as much as a pound and is as much as a foot in length

F. Prostaglandin.

- Prostaglandin hormones are injected into womb or released in
- Vaginal suppository cause uterus to contract and deliver baby prematurely
- Sometimes a saline solution is used to kill baby before the premature birth

G. RU 486

- Synthetic steroid used 5-7 weeks after conception
- Deprives baby of vital nutritional hormone progesterone
- Child starves to death as nutrient lining of the womb sloughs off
- Delivery of a dead baby

H. Partial-birth abortion

- Guided by ultrasound, the abortionist grabs the baby's legs with forceps
- The baby's leg is pulled out into the birth canal
- The abortionist delivers the baby's body, except for the head
- The abortionist jams scissors into the baby's skull. The scissors are then opened to enlarge the skull
- The scissors are removed and a suction catheter is inserted. The child's brains are evacuated out, causing the skull to collapse. The dead baby is then removed

> This quote found in a brochure at an OB-GYN office illustrates how abortion is viewed by many is our secular society today.
>
> "Every day we bear witness to each woman's knowledge of holding the profound power to decide whether or not to allow the life within her to come to term. The sharing of those moments makes abortion work sacred."
> -Merle Hoffman, owner of Choices Women's Medical Center in New York.

IV. The Key Questions: When does (a new) life begin?

- _Conception_ ?
- _Implantation_ ?
- _Brainwave Activity_ ?
- _Viability_ ?
- _Partial Birth_ ?
- _Birth_ ?
- _Personality Development_ ?

I am often asked, "But what about the birth control pill"? How does it work?

- Stage 1 - Prevent ovulation
- Stage 2 - Stop conception by thickening cervical mucus
- Stage 3 - Stop implantation – by thinning the uterine wall

V. Arguments that support that a new life begins at Conception.

A. Arguments from **SCIENCE**

"Many people mistakenly feel that abortion is a "religious" issue. But it is not. It is a scientific issue, and specifically, a biological issue."
(http://www.johnankerberg.org/Articles/apologetics/AP0805W3.htm)

Dr. Keith L. Moore, Professor and Chairman of the Department of Anatomy, University of Toronto - Essentials of Human Embryology states: "Human development is a continuous process that begins when an ovum from a female is fertilized by a sperm from a male. Growth and differentiation transform the zygote, a single cell… into a multicellar adult human being."
(Keith Moore and T.V. N. Persaud in The Developing Human *(7th edition, 2003) *the most widely used textbook on human embryology)*

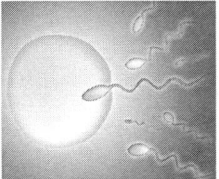

Chapter Three - Abortion

Professor Micheline Matthews-Roth, Harvard University Medical School:
"In biology and in medicine, it is an accepted fact that the life of any individual organism, reproducing by sexual production, begins at conception."
(http://topics.nytimes.com/top/reference/timestopics/subjects/a/abortion/index.html?s=oldest&offset=70&inline=nyt-classifier)

B. Arguments from the **SCRIPTURES**

- The ___unborn___ known by God (Jer 1:5, Ps. 139:13, Job 31:15)

    "Before I formed you in the womb I knew you, before you were born I set you apart; I appointed you as a prophet to the nations – Jeremiah 1:5.
    You made all the delicate, inner parts of my body and knit me together in my mother's womb" – Psalm 139:13.

- The life of the unborn is ___protected___ by the same punishment for injury or death as that of an adult (Ex 21:22-23)

    Now suppose two men are fighting, and in the process they accidentally strike a pregnant woman so she gives birth prematurely. If no further injury results, the man who struck the woman must pay the amount of compensation the woman's husband demands and the judges approve. But if there is further injury, the punishment must match the injury: a life for a life – Exodus 21:22-23.

- Christ was human from the point of conception (Matt 1:18, Luke 1:35)

- Unborn children possess ___personal___ characteristics such as sin (Ps. 51:5) and joy (Lk 1:41,44) that are distinctive of persons

- The unborn are called by God before ___birth___.
    Listen to me, all you in distant lands! Pay attention, you who are far away! The LORD called me before my birth; from within the womb he called me by name – Isaiah 49:1. (Genesis 25:22-23; Judges 13:2-7)

- ___Unborn___ babies are called "children".
    At the sound of Mary's greeting, Elizabeth's child leaped within her, and Elizabeth was filled with the Holy Spirit. When I heard your greeting, the baby in my womb jumped for joy – Luke 1:41, 44. (Exodus 21:22)

- The same Greek word (brephos) is used for a baby ___inside___ the womb and outside the womb.
    And you will recognize him by this sign: You will find a baby wrapped snugly in strips of cloth, lying in a manger – Luke 2:12.
    (Luke 1:41, 44; 2:16; 18:15; Acts 7:19; 2 Timothy 3:15)

Chapter Three - Abortion

VI. Arguing Abortion: (Pro & Con)

*"Now how should [the question of the personhood of the fetus] be decided? Is it a **legal** question, a **constitutional** question, a **medical** question, a **philosophical** question, a **religious** question, or what is it?"*
- **Justice Harry Blackmun (Chief Justice and author of opinion of the court for Roe v. Wade)**

What are the main arguments *for* abortion?

See Planned Parenthood's *Nine Reasons Why Abortions are Legal*
http://www.plannedparenthood.org/news-articles-press/politics-policy-issues/abortionaccess/nine-reasons-why-abortions-are-legal.htm

Four main areas for arguing the abortion question (against):

1. *A Legal Defense*

   Focus: To argue that in the event we are not sure that human life exists, legally, we should err on the side of protecting life, rather than taking it or even acting in way that may potentially result in its death.

   Rationale: All persons in the US have a constitutionally protected "right to life." The Supreme Court could not determine when personhood begins. From a legal standpoint, it is better to err on the side of life in order to protect it.
   The burden of proof should be with the life-taker, and the benefit of the doubt with the lifesaver.

   Responding to pro-choice claims:
   "Women have a legal right to control their bodies in whatever way they want."

   First - No one has an <u>unconditional</u> (unqualified) legal right to do with their body whatever they wish, especially if it threatens to harm or kill another person.
   Second - In pregnancy there are <u>two distinct bodies</u> (i.e. individuals) involved, not just one.

   "Well, I am against abortion, personally, but we should not seek to legally impose our personal morality on those who think otherwise."
   First - When it comes to the life and death of human beings, laws are constantly imposed on us regardless of our beliefs to the contrary. Laws do not prevent the activity from happening, but they no doubt curtail it.
   Second - Argument from analogy – "I don't believe in slavery, personally, and will never own a slave, but I would not want to legally impose my views about slavery on someone who does believe in it."

2. Philosophical Defense

Focus: To argue that if personhood does not begin at the moment of conception/fertilization, then our value as humans is not <u>intrinsic</u> How much is a human life worth, and when does it have such worth? If not from conception, then human worth becomes dependent upon some other humans' arbitrary, conflicting and changing definitions of personhood.

Rationale: Once human life has been devalued at one stage of development, then it is easy to devalue it at successive stages of development, and it becomes difficult to protect human life if someone in authority (with legal and political power) considers a life "not worth living." Remember: The defense of the unborn is, ultimately, the defense of the human race.

3. Medical Defense

Focus: To counter the pro-choice idea that the unborn are nothing more than another "part" of the mother's body, and thus she should be able to do anything with *her* body that she chooses. Emphasize the <u>individuality</u> of our prenatal existence.

Rationale: A consideration of every "milestone" of fetal development from conception to the status of so-called "viability," the point, at which humans are said, under current abortion law, to have a right to life, will clearly show our *individuality*. We are *never* merely a part of our mother's body, but a unique individual from the time of conception to the moment of live birth.

4. Biblical Defense

Focus: To show two things.
1) While the Bible does not explicitly state that the unborn are persons, or "created in the image of God" it consistently uses language that takes this notion for granted, making it unnecessary to argue the point.
2) While the Bible does not explicitly forbid "abortion," it does forbid murder on account of humans being created "in the image of God," and, as stated above, the unborn (including Jesus when He was a zygote, embryo, and fetus prior to birth) are assumed to be in the image of God (in Christ's case God incarnate).

(See prior notes: arguments From Scripture)

VII. A HELPING STRATEGY: *The Woman Considering an Abortion*

> *Taken from: The Billy Graham Workers Handbook.*
> *A copy of the entire handbook can be downloaded free in as a pdf file from:*
> <http://www.needhimresources.com/webtraining/documents/Billy_Graham_Handbook.pdf>

- Commend her for calling.
- Tactfully remind her that she quite possibly has strong feelings about the moral implications of abortion or she wouldn't have called.
- Avoid being judgmental about her situation.
- Question her about her feelings on abortion:
  - What promoted you to call about your problem?
  - What are your real feelings about abortion?
  - What have you heard from others, Christian or not regarding abortion?
- Whether or not she believes abortion is wrong, present the Scriptures given in class along with any others that you think would apply.
- Ask her to consider the alternatives.
- If she is concerned about not being able to care for or support the child, ask her to consider adoption.
- Ask her if she has ever received Jesus Christ as her Lord and Savior. If appropriate, present the gospel.
- Suggest that she start reading the Bible.
- Ask if she has a church home. She should try to identify with a Bible-teaching church where she can find fellowship and encouragement, and can grow in her faith.

VIII. The Woman Who Has Had an Abortion and Suffers from Guilt

- Encourage her by saying that she has made the right choice in seeking help. We care and want to help in any way we can. God has an answer to every human situation, and she can trust Him to work for her good.
- Don't make a moral issue of her situation; at the same time, don't minimize the seriousness of such a choice. The fact that she is willing to share her feelings of guilt is an indication that

God is speaking to her.

- Dwell on God's forgiveness for those who are willing to repent and confess their sins to the Lord. To the woman taken in the act of adultery, Jesus said, "Neither do I condemn you; go and sin no more" (John 8: 11).
- Should confession result, do not dwell on the past (Philippians 3: 13-14).
- Ask if she has ever received Jesus Christ as her personal Savior. If appropriate, present the gospel.
- Suggest that she seek fellowship with God through Bible reading and prayer. Forgiveness is immediate, but a sense of restoration and acceptance will come in due time. Through commitment to this important discipline of prayer and Bible study, she will grow in her relationship with God.
- Suggest that she seek, or restore, fellowship with a Bible-teaching church. There she can counsel with a pastor, hear God's Word taught, and find strength through Christian relationships.
- Pray with her. Ask God for forgiveness, commitment, and strength for the future.

Selected Scriptures for Healing

- Anger
  - Eph 4:26, 31-32
  - Heb 12:15

- Depression
  - Psalm 40:1-5, 8-17
  - Psalm 6

- Forgiveness
  - Psalm 32:1-5
  - Psalm 51:1-3
  - I John 1:9
  - II Cor 5:21
  - Col 3:12-13

- Peace
  - Col 3:
  - Matt 11:28-30

  - Isa 26:3-4

- Support
  - Gal 6:1-2
  - Psalm 27

- Perseverance
  - Heb 12:1-2
  - Gal 2:20
  - I Cor 6:11
  - Phil 3:13-14

Chapter Three - Abortion

Chapter Four

EUTHANASIA
Applying a Biblical Worldview

Duet 5:17 (NLT) *Do not murder.*

Job 1:21 (NKJV) *And he said: "Naked I came from my mother's womb, And naked shall I return there. The Lord gave, and the Lord has taken away; Blessed be the name of the Lord."*

II Cor 12:9 (NKJV) *And He said to me, "My grace is sufficient for you, for My strength is made perfect in weakness." Therefore most gladly I will rather boast in my infirmities, that the power of Christ may rest upon me.*

The term euthanasia is derived from the Greek prefix <u>eu</u>, meaning "good" or "easy," and the Greek noun <u>thanatos</u>, meaning "death." Today the word is used to denote the act of one person killing another because the person killed is terminally ill, suffering, disabled, or elderly.

I. Euphemisms

- Death w/ dignity
- Dying Gracefully
- "Compassion in Dying"
- "Planned Death"
- Good death

II. Prominent Names to Know

A. __Derek Humphry__ – head of Hemlock Society

B. __Jack Kevorkian__ – Dr. Death

C. __Karen Ann Quinlan__ – persistent vegetative state, taken off life support in 1976 and lived 10 more years

BIOGRAPHY

Dr. Jack Kevorkian

Born: 28 May 1928
Died: 3 June 2011
Birthplace: Pontiac, Michigan
Best known as: The euthanasia advocate known as "Dr. Death" Jack Kevorkian was the former medical pathologist known for his high-profile antics in support of voluntary euthanasia. A 1952 graduate of the University of Michigan medical school, Jack Kevorkian became known to colleagues as "Dr. Death" for his keen interest in dying patients. Dr. Kevorkian became famous in the 1990s for his "death machine," a device he invented that allowed a user to self-inject an anesthetic and then a lethal dose of potassium chloride. (He called the machine a *thanatron*, after Thanatos, the figure of death in Greek mythology.) He was convicted in April of 1999 and sentenced to 10-25 years in prison. Denied parole in 2005, Kevorkian, in failing health, was granted parole at the end of 2006 and released in 2007.

http://www.infoplease.com/biography/var/jackkevorkian.html Retrieved: December 2012

Chapter Four - Euthanasia

BIOGRAPHY

Terri Schiavo
Born: 3 December 1963
Died: 31 March 2005
Birthplace: Pennsylvania

On 25 February 1990, 26-year-old Terri Schiavo suffered severe brain damage when her heart stopped for five minutes. Schiavo spent the following years in rehabilitation centers and nursing homes but never regained higher brain function. In 1998 her husband, Michael Schiavo, filed a legal petition to have Schiavo's feeding tube removed, saying that his wife had told him before her medical crisis that she would not want to be artificially kept alive in such a situation. Terri Schiavo's parents, Bob and Mary Schindler, fought this request. Schiavo's feeding tube was removed in 2003, but reinserted six days later when the Florida legislature passed "Terri's Law," which allowed the state's governor to issue a stay in such cases. The law was later ruled invalid by the courts. In March of 2005 Schiavo's feeding tube was again removed, and the case became a greater public sensation when the U.S. Congress was called into special emergency session to pass a bill allowing federal courts to review the case, with President George W. Bush flying from Texas to Washington especially to sign the bill into law. However, federal judges and the U.S. Supreme Court refused to intervene. After two weeks without food and water, Schiavo died of dehydration on 31 March 2005.

http://www.infoplease.com/biography/var/terrischiavo.html   Retrieved: December, 2012

D. __Terry Schiavo__ – suffered severe brain damage in 1990. In 2005 her feeding tube was removed and she died 13 days later. (see Biography box to left)

Discuss –

III. Types of Euthanasia

1. __Passive__ Euthanasia

Withholding medical treatment or discontinuing treatment ..."letting die"...cause of death is the same as the condition causing the suffering (disease, respiratory failure, etc).

Is this really Euthanasia? –

2. __Active__ Euthanasia

Actively doing something to bring about the death of the patient...lethal injection, smothering with a pillow, etc....the cause of death is not the condition causing the suffering, but rather something else.

3. __Involuntary__ Euthanasia

Patient does not request their own death - someone else decides for them that they are better off dead. Usually when a patient is unable to communicate (coma) or unable to understand their condition.

4. __Voluntary__ Euthanasia

Patient requests their own death - either verbally, in writing or via a living will. (Some states will recognize testimony of family/friends, but not all)

Chapter Four - Euthanasia

These types combine to give us 4 Basic Forms of Euthanasia

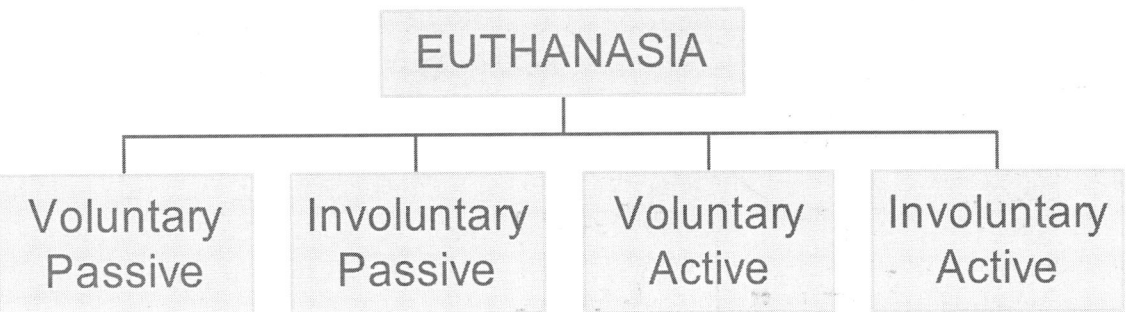

Physician-Assisted Suicide
This is a suicide in which a person's reasons for dying are similar to that of euthanasia. However, rather than take his or her own life, the person is assisted in the suicide by a physician.

Dr. Kevorkian

IV. Five Main Arguments Used To Promote Euthanasia

- Choice
- Control
- Compassion
- Cash
- Capability

THINKING

Question: What argument might you use that would allow for euthanizing animals but not humans? What is the key issue?

Question: What do you think about a DNR (Do Not Resuscitate) order? Dr. Matthews does not see this as euthanasia. What do you think… and why?

V. Commonly Used Defenses for Euthanasia

A. It is a __religious__ issue
B. Guidelines can prevent uses/abuses
C. It would only be for the "__hard cases__"
D. We euthanize __animals__ to relieve suffering, why not people?
E. There is no difference between "choice" in __abortion__ and "choice" in euthanasia
   (True or False?)

Chapter Four - Euthanasia

VI. Consequences

A. When life is devalued, it slowly depreciates further over time

"Protecting from one end of the age spectrum to the other, we see euthanasia for the elderly as the counterpart to abortion for the very young. There is no moral distinction between the two. Quality-of-life proponent Joseph Fletcher agrees: 'To speak of living and dying, therefore ... encompasses the abortion issue along with the euthanasia issue. They are ethically inseparable.' Those who take comfort in the fact that euthanasia is not practiced at present in America are leaning on a slim reed."

(Schaeffer, Francis, The Great Evangelical Disaster, Crossway, 1984)

B. __Quality of Life__ Ethic is Replacing a __Sanctity of Life__ Ethic

C. A __right__ to die will eventually be transformed into a __duty__ to die

D. The power to __choose__ will broaden from the individual to the "caregivers" to those "financially invested" to "institutions" and so on.

E. Options will become less available

F. Expanding expendability inevitable

VII. Traditional Arguments Against Euthanasia

A. __Expanding Expendability__
B. Physician/Patient relationship will weaken
C. __Quality of life__ ethic leads to some lives being deemed more __worthy__ than others
D. Abuses of the process & guidelines
E. Diagnoses and prognoses may be __wrong__
F. There will become a __duty to die__
G. Violation of the __Hippocratic Oath__

VIII. Biblical View of Euthanasia

A. Man is created in the **Image of God** (Gen. 1:26, James 3:9)

Then God said, "Let us make man in our image, in our likeness, and let them rule over the fish of the sea and the birds of the air, over the livestock, over all the earth, [a] and over all the creatures that move along the ground." – Genesis 1:26. Genesis 9:6.

Human life is **sacred** and should not be terminated merely because it is difficult (Sanctity of Human Life: Genesis 1_26-27, 9:6; Psalm 8:4-5, Isa 46:3-4, Psalm 139)

B. God is sovereign over life and death (Job 1:21; Ecc 3:1-2; Ps. 139:16)

See now that I myself am He! There is no god besides me. I put to death and I bring to life, I have wounded and I will heal, and no one can deliver out of my hand. – Deuteronomy 32:39.

C. Bible specifically condemns the taking of life (Ex. 20:13)

You must not murder – Exodus 20:13.

D. Our body as well as our spirit belongs to God (1 Co. 6:19-20)

Don't you realize that your body is the temple of the Holy Spirit, who lives in you and was given to you by God? You do not belong to yourself, 20 for God bought you with a high price. So you must honor God with your body – 1 Corinthians 6:19-20.

E. Suffering has a place in God's **dealings w/ man** (2 Co. 1:8)

And we know that in all things God works for the good of those who love him, who have been called according to his purpose – Romans 8:28.

F. As a result of the fall, **death** is inevitable (Ro. 5:12; 6:23)

Therefore, just as sin entered the world through one man, and death through sin, and in this way death came to all men, because all sinned – Romans 5:12.

G. We are responsible to care for the helpless and innocent. (Deuteronomy 14:29; Job 22:9)

Learn to do good. Seek justice. Help the oppressed. Defend the cause of orphans. Fight for the rights of widows – Isaiah 1:17.

Chapter Four - Euthanasia

6 CRITICAL CONCERNS REGARDING DECISION-MAKING AND THE END OF LIFE
(Integrating Biblical Theism with a modern ethical dilemma)

1. Our Presuppositions about God and Man

    A. Presupposition about God – Sovereignty of God – Deut 32:39, 1 Sam 2:6, Job 1:21

God alone is sovereign over life and death and alone has the prerogative to put to death, or order the death of, what He has created.

    B. Presupposition about Man – Sanctity of Life - All humans are persons from the moment of conception until the moment of cessation of life. (Genesis 1:27, Psalm 8:5-6; 139:14).

1) Sanctity of Life NOT Quality of Life – Intrinsic, not extrinsic value of human life.

2) Biological not Functional Criteria – Humanity is equated with personhood, or to be a human is to be a person, regardless of stage of development, age, or lack of physical or mental ability.

2. Our Primary Ethical Approach

    A. Deontological NOT Teleological (Utilitarianism) – "The ends and means must be just" (i.e. in line with God's revealed moral will) rather than "the ends justify the means."

    B. Responsibility to respect and protect human life (including one's own).

3. The Principle of Non-Malfeasance

    DO NO HARM – Romans 13:10 "Love does no harm to a neighbor" This encompasses killing (Exodus 20:13) – it is immoral (unloving) to:

1) Take another's life

2) Take one's own life (Note: all the cases in the Bible in which someone takes their own life occurs in a context of rebellion towards God. (Distinguish between suicide, sacrifice and martyrdom)

3) Assist another in taking their life.

Chapter Four - Euthanasia

NOTE: These first three principles rule out any kind of euthanasia from a Christian perspective.

Remember, "euthanasia" *is any act or omission that is intended to cause death.* **This does not, however, mean that we cannot allow death to occur at times, or aggressively treat pain.**

4. Our Perspective on Death

A. Biblical –

1) Death is *inevitable*, and thus *unavoidable*, for all: Job 14:5, Ecclesiastes, 3:2, Hebrews 9:27. - The certainty of death (death is unavoidable and inevitable) must be accepted. Death is not according to God's original plan, but since the fall, when "death came into the world" as a result of sin, it has been the common human experience. To realize that there is, in fact, a "time to die" is an important way to think when it comes to some tough end of life situations.

2) Death for the believer - Carries with it the certainty of eternal joy (Being "absent from the body and present with the Lord" is desirable over remaining in the body.) Yet, to remain in the body until the Lord takes us home is non-negotiable. As far as the believer is concerned death:

   a) Is *not to be feared*: 1 Corinthians 15:54-55, Hebrews 2:14

   b) Is *welcome* to the one who dies knowing Christ: (Psalm 116:15, John 11:25-26, 2 Corinthians 5:6-8, Philippians 1:21)

   c) Is *not to be hastened* (This would mean by another or one's self - Philippians 1:22-24, Implicit teaching of Proverbs 31:4-5)

3) Death for the unbeliever – Means not t the end of suffering, but rather the beginning of endless suffering (Revelation 20:11-15)

B. Biological –

1) *The physiology of dying* – a *process* in which the body gradually shuts down. This means that the body cannot, in cases of *the last stages of terminal illness* (not necessarily for coma or PVS patients), absorb food and water. It must be considered

that the administration of food and water may be causing more pain (doing more "harm" Romans 13:10) than helping someone live.

2) *The finality of death* - Uniform Determination of Death Act; **All four** criteria must apply:

A) Lack of response to external stimuli

B) Absence of spontaneous muscular movements and spontaneous respiration

C) No elicitable reflexes

D) Flat Electroencephalogram (EEG)

5. Palliative Care

Focus is upon *comfort* for the dying, not *cure* (Cf. Proverbs 31:6-7, but something should be given to the dying to ease (not hasten) the dying process. Measures should be taken to help them forget their pain and the misery of dying. (See below for more details)

6. The Principle of Double Effect

Giving enough medication to control severe pain may result in the patient's death. The key is that the ***intent*** is to kill the pain, not the patient, although it is fully known that the patient *may* die in the process.

IX. What Is Hospice and Palliative Care?

A. Help patients and families deal with the fear of the unknown

B. Help with pain control

"Palliative Care" is when the focus of medical goals and techniques is upon *comfort*, not *cure*. It emphasizes the alleviation of physical pain as well as the identification and meeting of emotional and spiritual needs fro the patient and family until the patient dies from the underlying disease process.

C. Thoughts of suicide and depression are dealt with

D. They deal with the "burden" issue

E. They help the family deal with the care of the dying

X. What Can We Do?

- Be Informed
    - Inform populace of alternatives
    - Inform people of the dangers of "cracking the door"
    - Train doctors in pain management
- Be Involved
- Be In Touch

Chapter Four - Euthanasia

Chapter Four - Euthanasia

Chapter Five

GENDER ISSUES
Applying a Biblical Worldview

Genesis 1:27 (NIV) *So God created man in his own image, in the image of God he created him; male and female he created them.*

Proverbs 31:10 (KJV) *Who an find a virtuous women? For her price is far above rubies.* (Just read the whole chapter! ☺)

Ephesians 5:24-25 (NLT) *As the church submits to Christ, so wives must submit to your husbands in everything. And you husbands must love your wives with the same love Christ showed the Church.*

Acts 18:26 (KJV) *And he (Apollos) began to speak boldly in the synagogue: whom when Aquila and Priscilla had heard; they took him unto them and expounded unto him the way of God more perfectly.*

I. Two Evangelical responses to the gender debates:

A. Egalitarianism (Biblical Feminism)

"Gender equity", "gender equality", "sexual equality", or **gender egalitarianism** is the belief in the equality of the gender or the sexes –

"The belief and interpretive framework that attempts to apply basic feminist ideas of equality to the Scriptures and thus the home and church. While rejecting the extremes of feminism, like an androgynous society, the tendency is to interpret Scripture as a "patriarchal" book limited to its time and culture. It focuses on the new ways in which women were being viewed and treated by Jesus and even suggested by Paul as totally equal to men in every way and not to be limited in terms of any ministry opportunities by their gender" *(GNED Professor, Liberty University, Dr. Will Honeycutt)*

B. Complementarianism

A view of the relationship between the genders that differs from gender equalism, in that it believes that both men and women are equal in status, but can have different and *complementary* roles –

Chapter Five – Gender Issues

"A response to biblical feminism to reaffirm that men and women are equal in essence or identity having been created in the image of God, but still have differing roles in the home and church based on gender distinctions created by God. With regard to these roles, in the home the man is to be the loving head of the woman, and the woman is to voluntarily submit to his leadership. In the church, God has ordained that men are to lead the church, and women are to support this work in the use of their gifts. There are God-ordained roles according to gender, and it is in fulfilling them that both men and women will find their greatest fulfillment in life."

(GNED Professor, Liberty University – Dr. Will Honeycutt)

II. A Biblical Approach to Gender Issues

A. Men and women in society

1. <u>Both</u> created in the image of God – Gen. 1:27
2. <u>Both</u> were to subdue and rule over everything on the earth – Gen. 1:28
3. <u>Both</u> could receive Spiritual gifts. – Rom 12; I Cor. 12
4. <u>Both</u> are spiritually equal in Christ – Galatians 3:28
5. <u>Both</u> could be business leaders in the community. – Prov. 31:10-31
   - There is NO reason why a woman cannot be a CEO etc...
   - There is NO reason why women shouldn't receive equal pay.

B. Men and women in the home

1. The role of the husband
   - Love his wife and sacrifice for her. – Eph. 5:25; Col. 3:19
   - Head of the wife. – Eph. 5:23,24; Titus 2:5, I Cor 11:3
   - Provide for his family. - I Tim. 5:8
   - Honor and respect wife. – I Peter 3:7
   - Provide a positive environment for children. – Col. 3:21
2. The role of the wife
   - Submit to her husband, (not to men in general). – Eph. 5:22-24; I Peter 3:1-6, I Cor 11:3

This is NOT what the Bible teaches when it says submit!!

"The principle of subordination and authority pervades the entire universe. Paul shows that woman's subordination to man is but a reflection of that greater general truth. Christ is the head of every man, and the man is the head of a woman, and God is the head of Christ. If Christ had not submitted to the will of God, redemption for mankind would have been impossible, and we would forever be doomed and lost. If individual human beings do not submit to Christ as Savior and Lord, they are still doomed and lost, because they reject God's gracious provision. And if women do not submit to men, then the family and society as a whole are disrupted and destroyed. Whether on a divine or human scale, subordination and authority are indispensable elements in God's order and plan." *(MacArthur, John F., 1 Corinthians: The MacArthur New Testament Commentary, (Chicago: Moody Press) 1984.)*

- Love her husband and children. – Titus 2:4
- Keep the family a priority. – Titus 2:5;   I Timothy 5:14

C. A Women's role in the church

1. What women can do.
   - Train younger women. – Titus 2:3-4
   - Teach children. – II Tim. 1:5, 3:15
   - Pray – I Cor 11:5
   - Singing – Col. 3:16 (nothing gender specific. Note v. 18)
   - Correct false teaching – Acts 18:26 (Aquila, Priscilla & Apollos)
   - Vote – Acts 1:14-26 (Women took part in voting for a replacement for Judas Iscariot)
   - Serve as Deaconess – Rom. 16:1,2 (Pheobe)

"Servant translates *diakonos*, the term from which we get deacon. The Greek word here is neuter and was used in the church as a general term for servant before the offices of deacon and deaconess were developed. It is used of the household servants who drew the water that Jesus turned into wine (John 2:5, 9), and Paul has used the term earlier in this letter (Rom. 13:4, twice) to refer to secular government as "a minister of God to you for good" and even of Christ as "a servant to the circumcision," that is, to Jews (15:8). When *diakonos* obviously refers to a church office, it is usually transliterated as "deacon" (see, e.g., Phil.1:1; 1 Tim. 3:10, 13).

In 1 Timothy 3:11, Paul declares that "women must likewise be dignified, not malicious gossips, but temperate, faithful in all things." Some argue that he is referring to wives of deacons, rather than to an office of women deacons. But it makes no sense that high standards would be specified for the wives of deacons but not for wives of overseers (or bishops, who are also called elders, see Titus 1:5), whose qualifications he has just given in verses 1–7. In this context (3:1–10, 12–13), the office of deaconess is clearly implied. The "likewise" in verse 11 ties the qualifications of these women to those already given for the offices of overseer and deacon. In verse 11, Paul did not refer to those women as deaconesses because *diakonos* has no feminine form." *(MacArthur, John F., Romans: The MacArthur New Testament Commentary, (Chicago: Moody Press) 1994.)*

2. What women cannot do.
   - Pastor of a church – I Tim. 2:11-14, 3:1-2
   - Rule in authority over a man. – I Tim. 2:11-14

2:11 Let a woman learn. Women are not to be the public teachers when the church assembles, but neither are they to be shut out of the learning process. The form of the Gr. verb translated "let … learn" is an imperative: Paul is commanding that women be taught in the church. That was a novel concept, since neither first century Judaism nor Greek culture held women in high esteem.

2:12 I do not permit. The Gr. word for "permit" is used in the NT to refer to allowing someone to do what he desires. Paul may have been addressing a real situation in which several women in Ephesus desired to be public preachers…Thus Paul is forbidding women from filling the office and role of the pastor or teacher. <u>He is not prohibiting them from teaching in other appropriate conditions and circumstances</u> (cf. Acts 18:26; Titus 2:3-4). **to have authority over.** Paul forbids women from exercising any type of authority over men in the church assembly, since the elders are those who rule (5:17). They are all to be men (as is clear from the requirements in 3:2,5).

(MacArthur, John F., Romans: The MacArthur New Testament Commentary, (Chicago: Moody Press) 1994.)

Can a woman be a better preacher or shepherd than a man?

Is it all right for a woman to speak from a church pulpit?

NOTE: The issue with the role of women is not about ability or value; it is about authority, as given by God.

Chapter Six

HOMOSEXUALITY
Applying a Biblical Worldview

Leviticus 18:22 (NLT) - *"Do not practice homosexuality; it is a detestable sin.*

Romans 1:26-27 (KJV) *For this cause God gave them up unto vile affections: for even their women did change the natural use into that which is against nature: And likewise also the men, leaving the natural use of the woman, burned in their lust one toward another; men with men working that which is unseemly, and receiving in themselves that recompense of their error which was meet.*

"All sexual sins (fornication, adultery, homosexuality etc.) represent an attempt by mankind to deviate from God's best and to trespass into dangerous areas."
Anderson p. 165

I. Homosexuality: What Does the Bible Say?

A. Homosexuality was considered a sin in the days of the __Patriarchs__.
   1. Gen 18:20 "their sin is very grievous"
   2. Gen 19:1-12 Sodom and Gomorrah
   3. cf Jude 7

B. Homosexuality was considered a "capital crime" in the __Mosaic Law__ Law.
   1. Lev. 18:22 "abomination" or "detestable"
   2. Lev. 20:13
   3. Note: __Moral laws v. ceremonial laws__

C. The __N.T.__ is clear in its condemnation of homosexual conduct.
   1. I Cor 6:9-10
   2. Rom 1:24-32

II. The Pro-Homosexual View of Bible Passages and a Response.

A. The sin of Sodom was not homosexuality but inhospitality. This is due to the interpretation of Yada. Gen. 19:5

THINKING

Response: The word "__YADA__" (know) (v.5) can, and usually does, simply mean to make one's acquaintance, but Lot, just four verses later, referred to his daughters as having never "known" a man (v.9)." This is clearly a reference to sexual intercourse, as is Genesis 4:1 and numerous other passages, particularly in Genesis.

> Much of the biblical rhetoric in support of homosexuality derives from the Metropolitan Community Church (MCC). Founded in 1968 by Troy Perry, their primary message is; "whoever you are, wherever you may be, whatever the circumstances of your life, it is important for you to know that Jesus died to take away your sins, not your sexuality. Christ accepts you as you are, and so do we. You are always welcome at MCC!" (April 1996 publication of the MCC entitled Sexuality and Scripture: Homosexuality in the Church). (Note: As of October, 7, 2005, he was replaced by Rev. Elder Nancy Wilson).
>
> **Question:** What parts of the statement of above would you agree or disagree with (and why)?

B. Some believe David and Jonathan were gay lovers (Also Ruth and Naomi, some will even suggest Jesus and John). I Samuel 18-20; key verses 18:3,4 20:41(KJV)

Response: Celebration of same-sex love does not mean that same-sex intercourse or sexual relations are being advocated!

C. Jesus never mentioned or condemned homosexuality.

Response: Not everything spoken by Jesus is recorded (John 21:24-25). Also note that there are many other things that Jesus did not mention. (E.g. rape, bestiality, slavery, drug abuse, the list goes on). Do we then conclude that since He did not say anything negative about these, they must therefore be permissible?
Response: Jesus did uphold the OT law (Matthew 5:17-19), repealing some of the ceremonial laws (Mark 7:18-19), but never a moral law.

D. I Corinthians 6:9 and I Timothy 1:9-10 only speaks against offenses i.e. improper homosexual activity. Paul was condemning the ancient Greek practice of pederasty (homosexual pedophilia) or male prostitution, not monogamous, committed homosexual relationships of which he and other biblical authors were ignorant.

<u>Response</u>: In these two passages Paul is making a reference to, and thus a ratification of, the OT laws of Leviticus (18:22, 20:13) which condemns all same-sex male-to-male intercourse.

III. A Christian Approach to Homosexuality.

◆ SPEAK THE **truth** IN **love**

 **THINKING**

Question: For arguments sake let's say that the headline in tomorrow's paper says that Doctors have proof that homosexuality is genetic (I am not suggesting they have or ever will). Would such a declaration change what the Bible says about homosexual acts?

Question: If something is legal, does that make it moral.

- *"speaking the truth in love"* (Eph 4:15).
- *"And a servant of the Lord must not quarrel but be gentle to all, able to teach, patient, in humility correcting those who are in opposition, if God perhaps will grant them repentance, so that they may know the truth, and that they may come to their senses and escape the snare of the devil, having been taken captive by him to do his will."* (2 Tim 2:24-26)

◆ HOMOSEXUALITY IS A **behavior** PATTERN THAT CAN BE **changed**.

- *"Do not be deceived: Neither the sexually immoral nor idolaters nor adulterers nor male prostitutes nor homosexual offenders… will inherit the kingdom of God. And that is what some of you were. But you were washed, you were sanctified, you were justified in the name of the Lord Jesus Christ and by the Spirit of our God"* I Cor 6:9-11

◆ **Help** THOSE WHO WANT TO **Overcome** HOMOSEXUALITY

- *"Brethren, if a man is overtaken in any trespass, you who are spiritual restore such a one in a spirit of gentleness, considering yourself lest you also be tempted. Bear one another's burdens, and so fulfill the law of Christ."* Galatians 6:1-2

Chapter Six - Homosexuality

What should be my attitude toward Homosexuality?

(Taken from: The Moral Catastrophe by David Hocking)

◆ Do not hate homosexuals; hate homosexuality and what it does to people.

◆ Never believe that "sexual preferences" should be added to our understanding and application of human rights or civil rights.

◆ Do not discriminate against homosexuals in terms of the rights to which all Americans are entitled, but never be intimidated or pressured to approve or accept their lifestyle and activity.

◆ Teach your children what the Bible says about sexual matters, and warn them of sexual sins (adultery, homosexuality etc)

◆ Do not treat homosexuality as a more terrible sin than adultery among heterosexuals, but never view it as harmless or tolerable.

◆ Encourage homosexuals to accept God's love and forgiveness in the work and person of Jesus Christ. Show them that God's power can give them the inner strength, courage, and desire not to be involved in homosexual activities.

◆ Make sure that your own personal beliefs, principles and lifestyle are in line with biblical morality. You should be committed to demonstrating that the only safe and right sex is between a husband and a wife.

FIGURE 1

Response: Homosexuality

Secondary cause: Sin

Primary cause: Biology or deficit in relationship with same-sex parent, low self-esteem, etc.

Common though unbiblical conceptualization of the development of homosexuality

FIGURE 2

Sinful practice: Homosexuality

Possible necessary influences: Genetics, peers, family, sexual violation by older person, etc.

Sufficient cause: sinful heart

Biblical conceptualization of the development of homosexuality

(Welch, Edward. Homosexuality: Current Thinking and Biblical Guidelines.
http://www.afa.net/homosexual_agenda/homosup.pdf)

IV. Myths Behind the Homosexual Agenda

A. Homosexuality qualifies for minority status and special legal protection.

1. Minority Status - (To achieve minority status, a group must fulfill three requirements, none of which are met by homosexuals.)

This is the logo used by "Soulforce" an organization whose purpose is to promote the acceptance of the homosexual lifestyle.

    i. Inability to succeed

    ii. Immutable (unchangeable) Characteristics

2. Political Powerlessness

    i. Response: They have not been denied the right to vote, access to public buildings, and restrooms, nor been legally segregated.

    ii. They have always exercised and independently funded powerful political campaigns and causes.

B. #2 - Homosexuals compose 10% of the population.

1. Response: This figure based on the now discredited Kinsey sex studies of 1948-1952. Even homosexual leaders have recognized this but still use it in their propaganda for recruitment.

2. Response: Later, more objective studies indicated that only 1% - 3% were homosexual.

C. #3 - Homosexuality is genetically determined, thus uncontrollable

1. Response: Although several studies have indicated that this may be the case, the fact still remains that there is no conclusive scientific evidence that this is true.

2. Response: Alcoholism and violent tendencies may be inherited traits, but this does not make discrimination against these acts wrong. Even some homosexuals are not going for the genetic determinism argument.

Chapter Six - Homosexuality

D. #4 - Homosexuals cannot change
   1. Response: There are too many former homosexuals who testify that they learned and then unlearned this behavior, while in it they were convinced they could not help themselves.
   2. Organizations for helping people change through the power of Christ.
       i. Organizations Ministering to Homosexuals
       ii. Exodus International: (CA) 415-454-1017
       iii. Homosexuals Anonymous: (PA) 215-376-1146
       iv. New Creation Ministries: (CA) 209-264-6125
       v. Regeneration (MD) 401-661-0284

(Howe, Richard., Homosexuality in America: Exposing the Myths. http://www.afa.net/homosexual_agenda/homosexuality.pdf)

Chapter Six - Homosexuality

Chapter Seven

DATING RELATIONSHIPS
Applying a Biblical Worldview

II Corinthians 6:14-15, (TLB). *"Don't be teamed with those who do not love the Lord, for what do the people of God have in common with the people of sin? How can light live with darkness? ... How can a Christian be a partner with one who doesn't believe?"*

I Thess 4:3-5, (TLB). *"For God wants you to be holy and pure and to keep clear of all sexual sin so that each of you will marry in holiness and honor--not in lustful passion as the heathen do, in their ignorance of God and his ways."*

II Timothy 2:22, (TLB). *"Run from anything that gives you the evil thoughts that young men often have, but stay close to anything that makes you want to do right. Have faith and love, and enjoy the companionship of those who love the Lord and have pure hearts."*

The Three Biggest Decisions of Your Life.

- Who will be my _Master_ ?
- What will be my _mission_ ?
- Who will I _marry_ ?

I. Dating Defined

1. A form of romantic courtship between two individuals who may or may not expect marriage. www.allwords.com

2. An engagement to go out socially with another person, often out of romantic interest. www.freedictionary.com

3. Dating is a stage in a relationship in which the two individuals involved get acquainted by doing activities together. Causal dating is the process in which people meet and go out together without any expectation of a long-term, committed relationship. When two people are casually dating, they are usually spending time together without an exclusive relationship or any agreement to date in the future. – www.ehow.com

Note: Do not get too caught up in the term "dating". Some people may choose, or prefer to use other terms that basically designate the same social activity.

Chapter Seven – Dating Relationships

II. Types of Dating

A. __Recreational__ or __Casual__ dating involves a relationship that revolves around an event. There is no commitment beyond the date.

B. __Attachment-oriented__ dating or serious dating involves some level of commitment. Dating revolves around their relationship rather than the event.

III. Purposes/Outcomes of Dating.

A. Recreation (is this good? Why or why not?)

B. To learn to listen

C. To get to know those of the opposite sex and to learn to relate to them as persons made in the image of God

D. To learn to see others as persons, not objects

E. To enable one to learn more about oneself, including strengths and weaknesses

F. __Preparatory__ socialization for marriage and family roles

G. To facilitate __husband/wife__ selection, discover the kind of person you will marry

See article by Gary Chapman - http://www.crosswalk.com/1302909/

> **THINKING**
>
> **Question:** Are there wrong or at least unwise reasons for dating?
>
> **Question:** Can you list any biblical principles that would apply to deciding who you choose to date?
> 1.
> 2.
> 3.
> 4.
>
> Note: Some people may not "date" at all… and that is fine too.

Seven Habits of Highly Defective Dating.

(Taken from Joshua Harris - - I Kissed Dating Goodbye)

1. Dating leads to __intimacy__ but not necessarily to __commitment__.
2. Dating tends to skip the "__friendship__" stage of a relationship.
3. Dating often mistakes a physical relationship for __love__.
4. Dating often __isolates__ a couple from other vital relationships.
5. Dating, in many cases, __distracts__ young adults from their primary responsibility of preparing for the future.
6. Dating can cause discontentment with God's gift of singleness. (a string of uncommitted relationships is not a gift)

Chapter Seven – Dating Relationships

7. Dating creates an artificial environment for evaluating another person's __Character__.

(My Note: While the above 7 CAN be true, it DOES NOT have to be that way)

IV. Pitfalls of Dating
   A. When the __physical__ aspect is dominant, the __social__, __intellectual__, and __spiritual__ elements of the relationship will suffer.
   B. The possibility of getting to serious to fast.
      (Friendship, Dating, Engagement, Marriage)
   C. Reputation – Prov 22:1, 2 Cor 6:41
   D. Flesh control – James 1:14-17
   E. __Lust__ (II Cor 6:14) __Modesty__ (I Tim 2:9)
   F. Breaking up is hard to do… and it hurts too.

How Far is to Far? - Is it?:

* All the Way (1 Cor 6:9-11)
* When it becomes lust (1 Thess 4:4-9)
* When one feels guilty (Romans 14:13-23)

THINKING

Question: As a Christian, are there right and wrong ways to break up?

Question: Can you list any biblical principles that would apply to how you might end a dating relationship?
1.
2.
3.
4.

"there are girls here on campus that you have no business dating, Lucas." -Matthews

= HAYLYNN GAUNT

Where will you draw the line? (Discuss)

No Physical Contact
  Holding Hands
    Light Touching
      Kissing
        Passionate Kissing
          Caressing, Fondling
            Sexual Intercourse

Chapter Seven – Dating Relationships

My Summary:
The issue has never been about _____. The issue is about _____.
The same standards of holiness that apply to you as single people, still apply to me as a married man. According to the Scriptures all sexual activity (activities meant to, or resulting in arousal of sexual desire) must be kept with in the confines of a marriage between a husband and wife.

V. Immoral Sex & Its Consequences

Hebrews 13:4 (NIV) - *Marriage should be honored by all, and the marriage bed kept pure, for God will judge the adulterer and all the sexually immoral.*

   A. God values _marriage_.
   B. Sex in marriage is morally _pure_.
   C. Sexual relations outside marriage are _immoral_.

CONSEQUENCES

1) Physical – Proverbs 5:11; 1 Corinthians 6:18
    i. Unplanned pregnancy
    ii. Sexually transmitted diseases (STD's))
        18.9 million new cases in 2000 (AGI)
        * Bacterial – treatable with antibiotics, but can be dangerous
            (Chlamydia, Syphilis, Gonorrhea)
        * Viral – not curable; can only be treated symptomatically.
            (Genital Herpes, Hepatitis, Human Papillomavirus (HPV), HIV/AIDS)
2) Emotional – Sex is more than a physical act – 1 Corinthians 6:16
    i. GUILT – Proverbs 5:11-14
    ii. Unwanted memories – Psalm 51:3
    iii. Feeling "dirty"
    iv. Anxiety and depression
    v. Fear of disease
    vi. Comparing sexual partners
3) Spiritual/Moral – 1 Peter 2:11
    i. Weakened conscience and moral resolve
    ii. Alienation from God – 1 Corinthians 6:9-10
    iii. Hindrance to fruitfulness in the Christian life

Chapter Seven – Dating Relationships

    iv. Less effective churches

  4) Social – someone always pays

    i. Children

    ii. Millions of dollars for medical costs and treatment of STDs

    iii. Abortions (and related consequences)

10 Ways to Practice Purity

(Campus Life – Jan/Feb 2001)

1. Keep innocent expressions innocent.

 (Rather than making innocent expressions a mere prelude to "heavier stuff.")

2. Pace you Passion.

 (Realize you are trying to remain pure all the way to your wedding day)

3. Don't feed fantasies.

 (Feeding your thought life with junk only makes it harder to remain pure)

4. Remember whose property you're touching.

 (That person belongs to God!)

5. Make a promise to God, and daily renew your commitment.

 (Seek God and draw the line, then keep it)

6. Acknowledge Jesus' presence on every date.

 (Start & finish your date with prayer)

7. Agree on your standards.

 (Talk about your standards/line together)

8. Don't always go it alone.

 (Be selective where – Spend time with others)

9. Put real love first. (always respects)

10. Declare a new beginning. (start now!)

VI. Biblical Principles to Apply when Dating *(Taken from: www.bibleinfo.com)*

- What kind of person should you date?

II Timothy 2:22, TLB. *"Run from anything that gives you the evil thoughts that young men often have, but stay close to anything that makes you want to do right. Have faith and love, and enjoy the companionship of those who love the Lord and have pure hearts."*

- Don't date someone who doesn't love God.

II Corinthians 6:14-15, TLB. *"Don't be teamed with those who do not love the Lord, for what do the people of God have in common with the people of sin? How can light live with darkness? ... How can a Christian be a partner with one who doesn't believe?"*
Amos 3:3 *"Can two walk together, unless they are agreed?"*

- Don't date someone who claims to be a Christian but doesn't live it.

I Corinthians 5:11, TLB. *"What I meant was that you are not to keep company with anyone who claims to be a brother Christian but indulges in sexual sins, or is greedy, or is a swindler, or worships idols, or is a drunkard, or abusive."*

- Inner beauty counts the most.

I Peter 3:4, TLB. *"Be beautiful inside, in your hearts, with the lasting charm of a gentle and quiet spirit that is so precious to God."*

- In a dating relationship don't be exclusive--care about others too.

Philippians 2:4, TLB. *"Don't just think about your own affairs, but be interested in others, too, and in what they are doing."*

- Let the relationship progress step by step.

II Peter 1:6-7, TLB. *"Next, learn to put aside your own desires so that you will become patient and godly, gladly letting God have his way with you. This will make possible the next step, which is for you to enjoy other people and to like them, and finally you will grow to love them deeply."*

* What to avoid on dates.

Romans 13:13, TLB. *"Be decent and true in everything you do so that all can approve your behavior. Don't spend your time in wild parties and getting drunk or in adultery and lust, or fighting, or jealousy."*

* Dating should not include a sexual relationship.

I Corinthians 6:13,18, TLB. *"But sexual sin is never right: our bodies were not made for that, but for the Lord...That is why I say to run from sex sin. No other sin affects the body as this one does. When you sin this sin it is against your own body."*
I Thess 4:3-5, TLB. *"For God wants you to be holy and pure and to keep clear of all sexual sin so that each of you will marry in holiness and honor--not in lustful passion as the heathen do, in their ignorance of God and his ways."*

CDC Releases Report on Sexual Behavior and Drug Use

Sunday, June 24, 2007

FOX NEWS

According to the U.S. Centers for Disease Control and Prevention, 96 percent of Americans over the age of 20 have had sex.

This is just one of the findings in a report issued Friday by the CDC's National Center for Health Statistics about American's sexual behavior and drug use.

The report uses data collected from 1999 to 2002 from 6,237 people aged 20 to 59. Participants submitted computer-assisted self-interviews about the use of cocaine, crack, freebase, and other street drugs, but marijuana was not included. Sexual behavior was defined as vaginal, oral or anal sex.

In previous federal surveys on these topics, participants were asked questions in face-to-face interviews; the CDC believes that caused underreporting of behaviors that might be viewed negatively.

"This is the first time we've used this technique," said Dr. Kathryn Porter, who served as medical officer for the survey. "The participants have a headset on, they hear questions, they touch the screen with responses. There's no one else in the room and they can take as long as they want."

Porter said the findings would provide grist for further studies, notably on the prevalence and patterns of sexually transmitted diseases.

Highlights from the report include:

• Twenty-nine percent of men reported 15 or more female sexual partners in a lifetime compared with 9 percent of women who reported having 15 or more male sexual partners in a lifetime.

• Of all race or ethnic groups, Mexican Americans had the highest percentage of persons never having sex at almost 12 percent.

• Sixteen percent of adults first had sex before the age of 15.

• Only 6 percent of non-Hispanic black persons abstained from sex until age 21 years and older compared with 17 percent for Mexican Americans and 15 percent for non-Hispanic white persons.

• The proportion of adults who first had sex before the age of 15 was highest for persons with less than a high school education

• The median number of lifetime female sexual partners for men was seven and the median number of lifetime male sexual partners for women was four.

http://www.foxnews.com/story/0,2933,286073,00.html

Chapter Seven – Dating Relationships

Chapter Seven – Dating Relationships

MARRIAGE & DIVORCE
Applying a Biblical Worldview

Matthew 19:4-5: (NLT) *Haven't you read," he replied, "that at the beginning the Creator 'made them male and female,' and said, 'For this reason a man will leave his father and mother and be united to his wife, and the two will become one flesh'?*

Eph 5:22,25,28 (KJV) *Wives, submit youselves unto your own husbands, as unto the Lord... Husbands love your wives, even as Christ also loved the church, and gave himself for it...So ought men to love their wives as their own bodies. He that loveth his wife loveth himself.*

Matthew 5:32 (KJV) *But I say unto you, That whosoever shall put away his wife, saving for the cause of fornication, causeth her to commit adultery: and whosoever shall marry her that is divorced committeth adultery.*

I. A Biblical View of Marriage

A. Marriage is between a male and a female.
   (Genesis 1:27-28; 2:21-24; Matthew 19:4-5)
B. Marriage involves a __Covenant__. (1Corinthians 7:2-4)
C. Marriage involves a _____ before God. (Matthew 19:6)
D. God is a witness of weddings, whether invited or not. (Matthew 19:6)
E. Husband and wife are literally joined together by God.

   Matthew 19:6: "So they are no longer two, but one. Therefore what God has joined together, let man not separate."

F. Marriage is a God-ordained institution for all people. It is the only social institution ordained by God before the fall of mankind. (Genesis 2:24-25)

II. Three Elements of Commitment

There is only one statement about marriage that God includes four times in the Scriptures.

"Therefore shall a man <u>leave</u> his father and his mother, and shall <u>cleave</u> unto his wife: and they shall be one flesh" (Gen 2:24, Matt 19:5, Mark 10:7-8, Eph 5:31)

Chapter Eight – Marriage & Divorce

A. "_Leaving_" – your parents
  1. What it does not mean
     a. That you totally forsake your parents (Ex 21:17, Mk 7:9-11, I Tim 5:4-8)
     b. That you must move 1000's of miles away. (It is possible to live two doors down and "leave", but it is also possible to be miles away and yet not "leave.")
  2. What it does mean.
     a. Establish an adult _relationship_ with them.
     b. You are more concerned about your _spouses_ ideas and approval.
     c. It means that you do not "run" to mom and dad every time have a problem.
     d. You make the husband/wife relationship your _priority_ in human relationships.

B. "_Cleaving_" – to your spouse
  1. Dict: _to adhere to, cling, be faithful_
  2. Society tells us that if it doesn't work to your _satisfaction_ then simply get out!
  3. God planned for marriage to last a _lifetime_. (Mark 10:7-9)
  4. Cleaving until "death do us part"

C. "WEAVING" – one flesh
  1. At its most elementary level this does refer to the sexual or physical union. (I Cor 6:16)
  2. It means more than just the marriage act! In a marriage relationship we share everything.
     a. _Body_
     b. _Money_
     c. _Dreams_
     d. _Cares & Struggles_
     e. _Your Life_

7 Keys to a Successful Biblically Based Marriage

1. **Christ** – Start with Christ at the centre of your relationship.
2. **Commitment** – To each other "til death do us part"
3. **Communication** – Honest and open.
4. **Cooperation** – Caring, considerate, working together as a team. As ONE flesh!
5. **Conflicts** – They will come so handle them with grace. Build don't tear down!
6. **Consummation** – Yes…the sexual element is also important.
7. **Church** – Again, emphasize the spiritual growth in the relationship.

III. God's Word on DIVORCE

REASONS FOR THE INCREASED DIVORCE RATE

- A Rise In **Individualism**: Concern has shifted from the well-being of families to personal happiness and success.

- **Romance** Only Lasts So Long: Society emphasizes a romantic love that can be replaced once the excitement is gone.

- Marriage Is **Stressful**: With both partners working (added stress)

- Divorce Is Socially Acceptable: Society encourages couples to divorce (Attitude)

- Legally A Divorce Is Easy To Obtain: Couples can divorce simply by showing their marriage has failed (Opportunity)

- Sexual **Promiscuity**: Physically and emotionally (includes pornography)

- **Materialism**: More effort is put into getting things, than working on a marriage

THINKING

There are studies that indicate a connection between involvement in many of the "social networks" (Facebook, Classmates.com etc.) and infidelity and divorce.
Question: How should we respond to the above statement/information?

Question: Give examples of choices that you might make today that could have major influence on your marriage in the future.
1.
2. Financial decisions (loans etc)
3.
4.
5.

Chapter Eight – Marriage & Divorce

KOALAFICATION

"In most states the classic grounds for divorce were cruelty, desertion, and adultery. This legal foundation changed when California enacted a statute in 1969 that allowed for no-fault divorce"
(Kirby Anderson, Moral Dilemmas, Word Publishers)

IV. Several Christian Views on Divorce

1. Christian Agreement on Divorce
   a. Divorce is not __God's ideal__ Malachi 2:16; Matthew 19:6,8
   b. Divorce is not permissible for every __cause__. Matthew 19:3,9
   c. Divorce creates many problems.

2. Christian Disagreement on Divorce
   a. Some will say there are __no__ __grounds__ for divorce.
      - Divorce violates God's design for marriage.
      - Divorce breaks a vow made before God.
      - Jesus condemned all divorce. (Mk 10:1-9; Luke 16:18)
      - The apostle Paul condemned divorce. (I Co 7:10-13)
      - Divorce disqualified an elder. (1 Timothy 3:2)
      - Divorce violates a sacred typology. Eph. 5:32 (God takes a violation of a sacred type seriously. See Numbers 20:9-12)

   b. Others will contend that there is only __1__ ground for divorce.
      - Jesus mentions __adultery__ as grounds for divorce. (Mt 19:9)
      - Jesus repeated this exception in a parallel passage. (Mt 5:32)
      - Paul agreed with Jesus' view on divorce. (1 Co 7:10,15)

   c. Still others hold that there are __many__ grounds for divorce.
      - Paul approves of divorce for __desertion__. (1Co 7:15)
      - Even God "divorced" Israel for unfaithfulness. (Jer. 3:8; Isaiah 50:1)
      - The Bible recognizes human frailty.
      - Failing to allow divorce is legalistic. (Mk 2:27)
      - Repentance changes the situation. There is only one unpardonable sin (Mt 12:32), and it is not divorce.

THINKING

Question: Looking back at the Scriptures, can a pastor be divorced?

Question: How should we respond to divorcees?

Question: How can the church help divorcees?

(See the class activity for further investigation of the issue as it relates to those in ministry positions)

CLASS ACTIVITY
You have been selected by the members of your church to deal with problems regarding divorced people and the issue of divorce.

1. List (as many as you can) problems that the church may be dealing with that involve the area of divorce.

2. List (as many as you can) reasons often given for divorce.

3. What does Scripture say about divorce?

4. In addition to the verses specifically mentioning divorce, what other Scriptures might be used in a discussion on divorce and why would they be used?

5. As a group develop a statement and policy on the issues of divorce and divorced people in your church.

Chapter Eight – Marriage & Divorce

Chapter Nine

RACIAL ISSUES
Applying a Biblical Worldview

I Corinthians 12:13 (TLB) *Some of us are Jews, some are Gentiles, some are slaves, and some are free. But we have all been baptized into Christ's body by one Spirit, and we have all received the same Spirit.*

Galatians 3:28 (TLB) *There is no longer Jew or Gentile, slave or free, male or female. For you are all Christians--you are one in Christ Jesus.*

Acts 10:34,35 (NIV) *Then Peter began to speak: 'I now realize how true it is that God does not show favoritism but accepts men from every nation who fear Him and do what is right.*

Acts 17:26 (KJV) *And has made of one blood all nations of men for to dwell on all the face of the earth.*

John 3:16 (NKJV) *For God so loved the world that He gave His only begotten Son, that whoever believes in Him should not perish but have everlasting life.*

RACISM Defined :

1. a belief that <u>race</u> is the primary <u>determinant</u> of human traits and capacities and that <u>racial</u> differences produce an inherent superiority of a particular race
2. racial <u>prejudice</u> or discrimination

http://www.merriam-webster.com/dictionary/racism

 **THINKING**

Question: Is racism still present in society today?

Question: How do you see racism expressed in America?

Question: How do you see racism expressed in other nations?

Question: In what ways do churches struggle with racism?

Question: Why do we have racism?

I. How is Racism Manifested?

A. __Stereotyping__ – A (usually negative) overgeneralization about a certain people group as a whole based on the unaccepted behavior of a few members of that group.

B. __Prejudice__ – "Prejudging" an individual in a negative way because he/she happens to be from a stereotyped group.

Chapter Nine – Racial Issues

C. __Discrimination__ – Unequal treatment of a person on the basis of his/her people group membership.

D. __Hate/speech crimes__ – Verbal and physical abuse directed toward people. This is considered justified on the basis of their group membership.

E. Genocide – Deliberate and systematic killing of an entire race or ethnic group, usually based on the belief that the ones being killed are evil/worthless and have no right to life.

II. What is Racism Based on?

A. Irrational Beliefs - That a certain people group as whole is intellectually or morally inferior

B. Pride (Ethnocentrism) - Especially in inherited traits and culture

(See I Corinthians 4:7).

1. Ethnocentricity "is the tendency to look at the world primarily from the perspective of one's own ethnic culture".

2. ETHNOCENTRISM [ethnocentrism] "the feeling that one's group has a mode of living, values, and patterns of adaptation that are superior to those of other groups. It is coupled with a generalized contempt for members of other groups. Ethnocentrism may manifest itself in attitudes of superiority or sometimes hostility. Violence, discrimination, proselytizing, and verbal aggressiveness are other means whereby ethnocentrism may be expressed" *(Encyclopedia.com)*

C. Ignorance

1. Educational

"the evolutionary view that life can evolve to "higher" levels provides fuel for racist ideas. The Bible on the other hand, clearly shows the fallacy of racism… this misleading concept gives rise to the idea that some "races" have developed and become more sophisticated faster than others, leading to the ultimate conclusion (often subconsciously) that certain "races" are superior" "

(Creation Ex Nihilo 20 Dec 97)

2. Voluntary

D. Fear
1. Of unknown
2. Of what is different

E. Socialization
1. Parental example
2. Uncritically accepted social assumptions

III. Combating Racism with Biblical Truth

A. Abrahamic Covenant – Genesis 12:1-3, 15:5-6, Romans 4:17-18; Gal 3:26-29

B. Mosaic Law – Exodus 23:9

C. Jesus' Example – John 4:1-10 (The Samaritan Women at the well)

D. Jesus' Teaching – Luke 10:25-37 (Parable of the Good Samaritan)

E. The Gospel breaks down divisive barriers and unifies races –
Acts 15:7-9, Rom 1:14-16, I Cor 12:13, Gal 3:28, Eph 2:13-20, Col 3:10-15

F. Heaven will be a multicultural celebration of Christ!!   - Rev 5:9-10

"Personally, because of the influences of Darwinian evolution and the resulting prejudices, I believe everyone (and especially Christians) should abandon the term "race(s)." We could refer instead to the different "people groups" around the world."

- Ken Ham "Are there really Differences in Races" http://www.answersingenesis.org/articles/nab/are-there-different-races. Retrieved December 11, 2012

Chapter Nine – Racial Issues

Racism – *(Taken from: www.bibleinfo.com)*

- _We are all one in Christ_.

    Galatians 3:28 (TLB) *"We are no longer Jews or Greeks or slaves or free men or even merely men or women, but we are all the same--we are Christians; we are one in Christ Jesus."*

- _Racism Bad_ Sin.

    James 2:8-9, NIV. *"If you really keep the royal law found in Scripture, 'Love your neighbor as yourself,' you are doing right. But if you show favoritism, you sin and are convicted by the law as lawbreakers."*

- All men have the same _blood_.

    Acts 17:26, KJV. *"And has made of one blood all nations of men for to dwell on all the face of the earth."*

- God accepts people from every _____, _____ and _____.

    Acts 10:34,35, NIV. *"Then Peter began to speak: 'I now realize how true it is that God does not show favoritism but accepts men from every nation who fear Him and do what is right.'"*

IV. Key Issues For The Church

   A. Interracial Marriage

     1. Marry _believers_ - 1 Corinthians 7:39.

     2. What is a _mixed_ marriage? - Deuteronomy 7:3-4; Exodus 12:48-49; 2 Corinthians 6:14; Colossians 3:9-11.

     3. What are some questions to ask?

       - What are your cultural differences?

- What do your families think about the marriage?
- What are the consequences for your children?

4. Notice Numbers 12:1, 10.

5. *What does the Bible say about the problems of interracial marriages?*

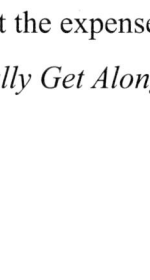

B. Racial __Unity__ among believers

1. Why do believers of different races struggle to be in the same church together?
2. There are cultural differences, but they must not be practiced at the expense of unity.
3. Obstacles that block progress *(from Tony Evans – Can We Really Get Along? – an article taken from his book <u>Let's Get To Know Each Other</u>)*
    a. Our fear of losing our racial distinction
    b. Our cultural prejudice
    c. Our fear of the price tag of unity
    d. Our hesitancy to hold people accountable for racial prejudice
4. Jesus' example in John 4.
5. Our priority - John 13:34-35; Luke 10:30-37; James 2:1-13.

"The church could greatly relieve the tensions over racism (particularly in countries like America), if only the leaders would teach that: all people are descended from one man and woman; all people are equal before God; all are sinners in need of salvation; all need to build their thinking on God's Word and judge all their cultural aspects accordingly; all need to be one in Christ and put an end to their rebellion against their Creator."

- Ken Ham "Inter-racial Marriage: Is it Biblical.

http://www.answersingenesis.org/articles/cm/v21/n3/inter-racial-marriage

. Retrieved December 11, 2012

 **THINKING**

Question: Ever heard of the "Curse of Ham"?
Unfortunately, an extreme and clearly erroneous interpretation of Genesis 9:18-27, 10:6 has been used by many within the church to justify racist beliefs.
Two good sources that explain the truth and the meaning of this passage are:
1. Kerby Anderson – "Race and Racial Issues" www.probe.org
2. Ken Ham ' "The Curse of Ham – It's Not True" www.answersingenseis.org

Chapter Nine – Racial Issues

Chapter Nine – Racial Issues

Chapter Ten

ALCOHOL & DRUG ABUSE
Applying a Biblical Worldview

Proverbs 23:29-35 (KJV) *23:29 Who has woe? Who has sorrow? Who has contentions? Who has complaints? Who has wounds without cause? Who has dullness of the eyes? (30) Those who linger over wine, those who go looking for mixed wine. (31) Do not look on the wine when it is red, when it sparkles in the cup, when it goes down smoothly. (32) Afterwards it bites like a snake, and stings like a viper. (33) Your eyes will see strange things, and your mind will speak perverse things. (34) And you will be like one who lies down in the midst of the sea, and like one who lies down on the top of the rigging. (35) You will say, "They have struck me, but I am not harmed! They beat me, but I did not know it! When will I awake? I will look for another drink."*

Eph 5:*18* *"And be not drunk with wine wherein is excess, but be filled with the Spirit"*

I. The Top Ten Misused Drugs

1. ___tobacco___ : biggest killer (400,000 deaths/year)
2. ___Alcohol___ : most widely abused legal substance
3. PRESCRIPTION DRUGS : dangerously addictive, rising in popularity
4. METHAMPHETAMINE : become a drug of choice, meth labs seizures up
5. MARIJUANA : most widely abused illegal substance
6. MDMA (ECSTASY) : little research on long term effects, still popular
7. CRACK COCAINE : cheap, destructive drug making a comeback
8. HEROIN : highly addictive drug making a comeback in some areas
9. ___Steroids___ : horrible side effects, the toll they're taking on athletics
10. INHALANTS : abuse is on the rise among youth again

(Taken from: www.streetdrugs.org/topten.htm

"A major source of information on substance use, abuse, and dependence among Americans aged 12 and older is the annual National Survey on Drug Use and Health (NSDUH) conducted by the Substance Abuse and Mental Health Services Administration. Following are facts and statistics on substance use in America from 2010, the most recent year for which NSDUH survey data have been analyzed."
http://www.drugabuse.gov/publications/drugfacts/nationwide-trends

Chapter Ten – Alcohol/Drugs

II. Statistics for Drug Use and Abuse
http://www.drugabuse.gov/publications/drugfacts/nationwide-trends

A. **Illicit drug use in America has been increasing.** In 2010, an estimated 22.6 million Americans aged 12 or older—or 8.9 percent of the population—had used an illicit drug or abused a psychotherapeutic medication (such as a pain reliever, stimulant, or tranquilizer) in the past month. This is up from 8.3 percent in 2002. The increase mostly reflects a recent rise in the use of marijuana, the most commonly used illicit drug.

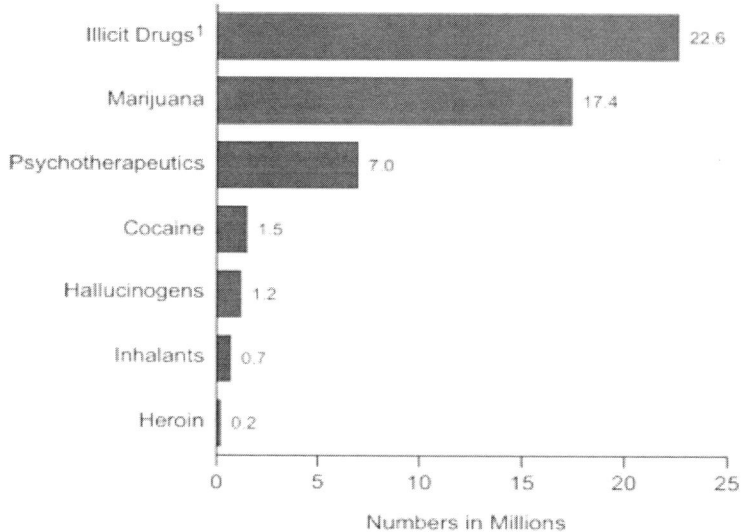

B. **Most people use drugs for the first time when they are teenagers.** There were 3.0 million new users (initiates) of illicit drugs in 2010, or about 8,100 new users per day.

C. **More than half of new illicit drug users begin with marijuana.** Next most common is prescription pain relievers, followed by inhalants (most common among younger teens)

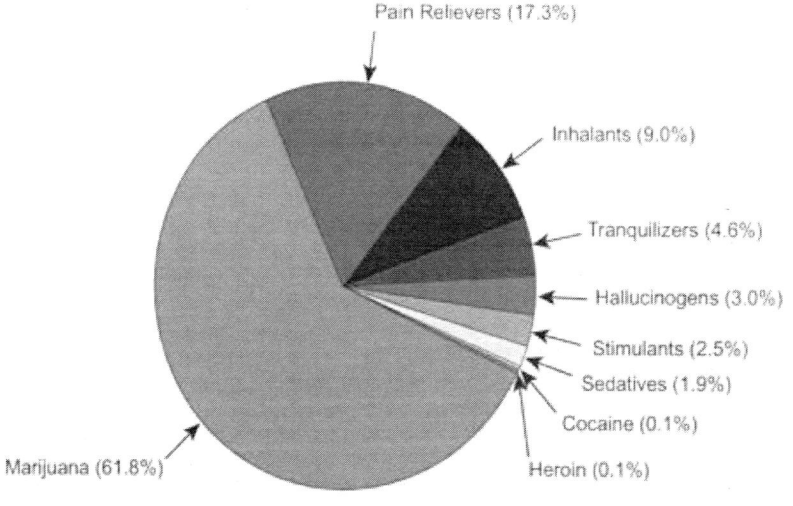

Chapter Ten – Alcohol/Drugs

D. Drug use is highest among people in their late teens and twenties. In 2010, 23.1 percent of 18- to 20-year-olds reported using an illicit drug in the past month.

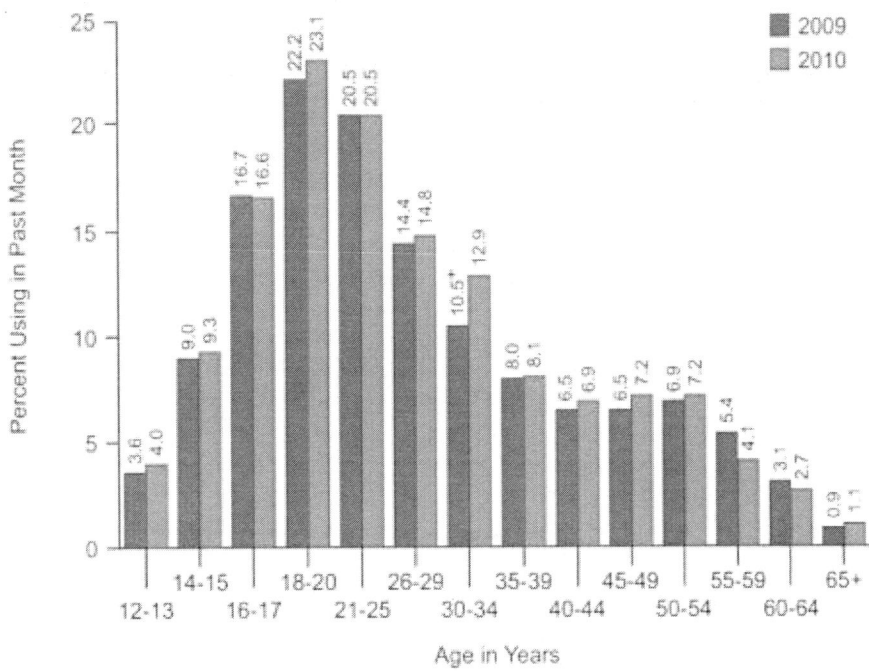

E. Fewer Americans are smoking. In 2010, an estimated 58.3 million Americans aged 12 or older, or 23 percent of the population, were current (past month) cigarette smokers. This reflects a continual but slow downward trend from 2002, when the rate was 26 per-cent.

F. Teen smoking is declining more rapidly. The rate of past-month cigarette use among 12- to 17-year-olds went from 13 percent in 2002 to 8.3 percent in 2010.

For more information on drug use among adolescents, see Drug Facts: High School and Youth Trends.

III. Statistics for Alcohol Use and Abuse

National Institute on Alcohol Abuse and Alcoholism:

"The tradition of drinking has developed into a kind of culture—beliefs and customs—entrenched in every level of college students' environments. Customs handed down through generations of college drinkers reinforce students' expectation that alcohol is a necessary ingredient for social success. These beliefs and the expectations they engender exert a powerful influence over students' behavior toward alcohol.
Customs that promote college drinking also are embedded in numerous levels of students' environments.

Chapter Ten – Alcohol/Drugs

Students derive their expectations of alcohol from their environment and from each other, as they face the insecurity of establishing themselves in a new social milieu. Environmental and peer influences combine to create a culture of drinking. This culture actively promotes drinking, or passively promotes it, through tolerance, or even tacit approval, of college drinking as a rite of passage."

(Taken from: http://www.collegedrinkingprevention.gov)

Current, Binge, and Heavy Alcohol Use among Persons Aged 12 or Older, by Age: 2010
U.S. Department of Health and Human Services Substance Abuse and Mental Health Administration

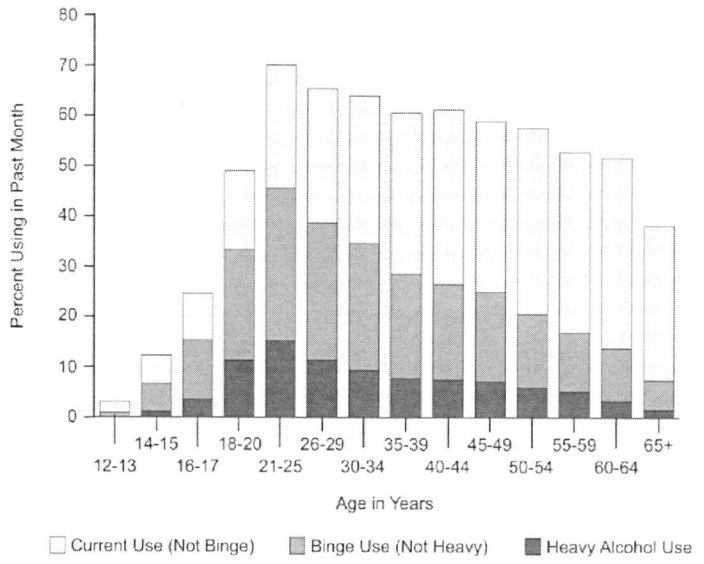

Binge Alcohol Use among Adults Aged 18 to 22, by College Enrollment: 2002-2010
U.S. Department of Health and Human Services Substance Abuse and Mental Health Administration

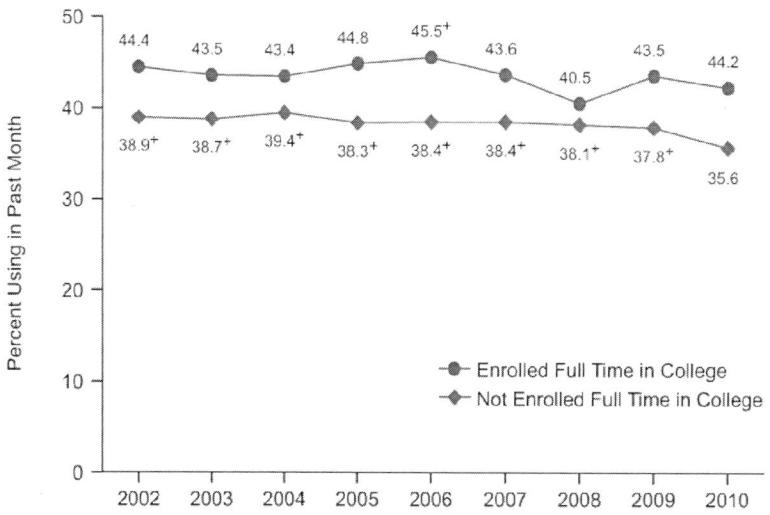

Chapter Ten – Alcohol/Drugs

A. **Drinking by underage persons (ages 12–20) has declined.** Current alcohol use by this age group declined from 28.8 to 26.3 percent between 2002 and 2010, while binge drinking declined from 19.3 to 17.0 percent and the rate of heavy drinking went from 6.2 to 5.1 percent.

B. **Binge and heavy drinking are more prevalent among men than among women.** In 2010, 30.9 percent of men 12 and older and 15.7 percent of women reported binge drinking (five or more drinks on the same occasion) in the past month; and 10.1 percent of men and 3.4 percent of women reported heavy alcohol use (binge drinking on at least five separate days in the past month).

C. **Driving under the influence of alcohol has also declined slightly.** In 2010, an estimated 28.8 million people, or 11.4 percent of persons aged 12 or older, had driven under the influence of alcohol at least once in the past year, down from 14.2 percent in 2002. Although this decline is encouraging, any driving under the influence remains a cause for concern.

http://www.drugabuse.gov/publications/drugfacts/nationwide-trends

D. Driving under the Influence Statistics (Center for Disease Control- CDC)

1. Every day, almost 30 people in the United States die in motor vehicle crashes that involve an alcohol-impaired driver. This amounts to one death every 48 minutes.

2. The annual cost of alcohol-related crashes totals more than $51 billion.2

3. In 2010, 10,228 people were killed in alcohol-impaired driving crashes, accounting for nearly one-third (31%) of all traffic-related deaths in the United States.1

http://www.cdc.gov/motorviclesafety/impaired_driving/impaired-drv_factsheet.html

IV. Alcohol and the Christian

A. You cannot compare drinking alcohol today to drinking alcohol in __biblical__ times. (1 part wine to 3 parts water) Therefore it cannot be used for justification of drinking.

B. __Drunkenness__ is wrong/sin – Galatians 5:19-21 - *Now the works of the flesh are evident: sexual immorality, impurity, sensuality, idolatry, sorcery, enmity, strife, jealousy, fits of anger, rivalries, dissensions, divisions, envy, drunkenness, orgies, and things like these. I warn you, as I warned you before, that those who do such things will not inherit the kingdom of God.* See also Deuteronomy 21:18-21; 1 Corinthians 6:9-11

C. Clear-mindedness is the standard – 1 Peter 5:8 - *Be sober-minded; be watchful. Your adversary the devil prowls around like a roaring lion, seeking someone to devour.* See also Luke 22:34-36; 1 Peter 1:13

D. There is no clear command for _total abstinence_ for believers. (i.e.; medicinal - Proverbs 31:6 - *Give strong drink to the one who is perishing, and wine to those in bitter distress.* 1 Timothy 5:23 - *No longer drink only water, but use a little wine for the sake of your stomach and your frequent ailments.*

E. General warnings in Scripture are against drinking; they are not neutral - Proverbs 20:1 - *Wine is a mocker, strong drink a brawler, and whoever is led astray by it is not wise.* See also Proverbs 23:30-33.

> **THINKING**
>
> Jesus's first miracle was turning the water into wine (John 2).
> **Question:** Was the "wine" a grape juice or did it have any alcoholic content? Can we tell? Does it matter?
>
> **Question:** Does the context of the story indicate anything?
>
> **Question:** What can we learn from other passages of Scripture where "wine" is used? (Does it refer to non-alcoholic and/or alcoholic beverages?)

F. Principle of brotherly love - Causing your brother to _stumble_ - Romans 14:21 - *It is good not to eat meat or drink wine or do anything that causes your brother to stumble.*

G. In the U.S. drinking is a sin (also a crime) for anyone under the age of _21_ - 1 Peter 2:13-15 - *Be subject for the Lord's sake to every human institution, whether it be to the emperor as supreme, or to governors as sent by him to punish those who do evil and to praise those who do good. For this is the will of God, that by doing good you should put to silence the ignorance of foolish people.*

H. Freedom can become a _sin_ if it breaks institutional rules (i.e., parents' rules, Liberty Way) - 1 Peter 2:13-15.

I. Those dedicated to God's service should abstain - Numbers 6:2-3; Leviticus 10:9; Ezekiel 44:21; Judges 13:4-5; Proverbs 31:4-5; Luke 1:15. It is interesting to remember - believers are a priesthood 1 Peter 2:9.

J. Everything a believer does should be done to the "_glory_ of God" - 1 Corinthians 10:31 - *So, whether you eat or drink, or whatever you do, do all to the glory of God.*

V. Why Christians Need Not Drink Alcohol - Norman Geisler

A. People today have plenty of wholesome, non-addictive beverages.

B. We live in an alcoholic culture.

C. Abstinence is the safer policy.

D. Abstinence is a more consistent policy.

(See Norman Geisler's article (A Christian Perspective on Wine-Drinking" - http://therev.home.mindspring.com/studies/wine.pdf)

What the Bible Says About Drinking Wine or Other Strong Drink

I. Uses of Wine in the Bible
   A. Wine was made from grapes (Gen. 40:11; 49:11) and pomegranates (Song 8:2).
   B. Wines were used at meals (Gen. 27:25; Matt. 26:27-29; Mark 14:23).
   C. Jesus made wine at the marriage feast in Cana (John 2).
   D. Wine was used for medicinal purposes (Prov. 31:6-7; I Tim 5:23).
   E. Melchizedek gave wine to Abraham (Gen. 14:18).
   F. Wine was offered with sacrifices (Ex. 29:40; Lev. 23:13; Num. 15:5, 10; 28:7, 14).
   G. Cheap wine (like vinegar) was given to Jesus at the crucifixion (Matt. 27:48; Mark 15:23; Luke 23:36; John 19:29).
   H. Wine was used in communion in the early church (I Cor. 11:21-22).
   I. Wine was used figuratively of:
      1. Divine judgments (Psa. 60:3; 75:8; Jer. 51:7)
      2. Of the joy of wisdom (Prov. 9:2,5)
      3. Of the joys of spiritual matters (Isa. 25:6; 55:1; Joel 2:19)
      4. Of abominations (Rev. 14:8; 16:19)

II. Warnings Against Drunkenness
   A. Overseers must not be given to drunkenness (I Tim. 3:3; Titus 1:7).
   B. Deacons are not to be indulging in much wine (I Tim. 3:8).
   C. Believers are not to be controlled by wine (Eph. 5:18).
   D. Older women are not to be addicted to much wine (Titus 2:3).

III. Sobriety (Clear-mindedness)
   A. Commanded (I Pet. 1:13; I Pet. 5:8)
   B. The Gospel is designed to teach sobriety (Titus 2:12).
   C. Sobriety is linked to watchfulness (I Thess. 5:6).
   D. Sobriety is necessary to be able to pray (I Pet. 4:7).
   E. Sobriety is required in:
      1. God's servants (I Tim. 3:2-3; Titus 1:8; 2:12)
      2. Wives of servants of God (I Tim. 3:11)
      3. Aged men (Titus 2:2)
      4. Young men (Titus 2:6)
      5. Young women (Titus 2:4)
      6. All saints (I Thess. 5:6,8)
   F. We should estimate our character and talents with sobriety. (Rom. 12:3)
   G. We should live in sobriety. (Titus 2:12)
   H. The motives of sobriety (I Pet. 4:7; 5:8)

IV. Instances of Drunkenness
   A. Noah (Gen. 9:21)
   B. Lot (Gen. 19:13)
   C. Nabal (I Sam. 25:36)
   D. Uriah (II Sam. 11:13)
   E. Elah (I King 16:9)
   F. Ben-hadad and his thirty-two confederate kings (I Kings 20:16)
   G. Ahasuerus (Est. 1:10-11)
   H. Belshazzar (Dan. 5:1-6)
   I. Priests during Isaiah's time (Isa. 28:7)
   J. Church of Corinth (I Cor. 11:21-22)
   K. Falsely Accused
      1. Hannah (I Sam. 1:12-16)
      2. Jesus (Matt. 11:19)
      3. The Apostles (Acts 2:13-15)

V. General Warnings About Drinking
   A. Proverbs 20:1
   B. Proverbs 21:17
   C. Proverbs 23:20
   D. Proverbs 23:30-31
   E. Romans 14:19-23
   F. I Corinthians 10:31

VI. Abstinence Demanded
   A. Nazarites (Num. 6:2-3); (Samson, Samuel, John the Baptist)
   B. Priests while on duty (Lev. 10:9; Ezek. 44:21) See Lev. 10:1-8
   C. Samson's mother (Judges 13:4-5)
   D. Rulers (Prov. 31:4-5)
   E. John the Baptist (Luke 1:15)

VII. Abstinence Practiced
   A. Daniel (Dan. 1:5,8,16; 10:3)
   B. Courtiers of Ahasuerus (Est. 1:10-11)
   C. Timothy (I Tim. 5:23)
   D. John the Baptist (Luke 1:15)

Chapter Eleven

POVERTY & the POOR
Applying a Biblical Worldview

Proverbs 14: 20,21,31 *(20) The poor is hated even of his own neighbor: but the rich hath many friends. (21) He that despises his neighbor sinneth: but he that hath mercy on the poor, happy is he. (31) He that oppresses the poor reproaches his Maker: but he that honoureth him hath mercy on the poor.*

Matthew 25:31-46 *(35) For I was an hungered, and ye gave me meat: I was thirsty, and ye gave me drink: I was a stranger, and ye took me in:*

Galatians 2:10 (NLT*) The only thing they suggested was that we remember to help the poor, and I have certainly been eager to do that.*

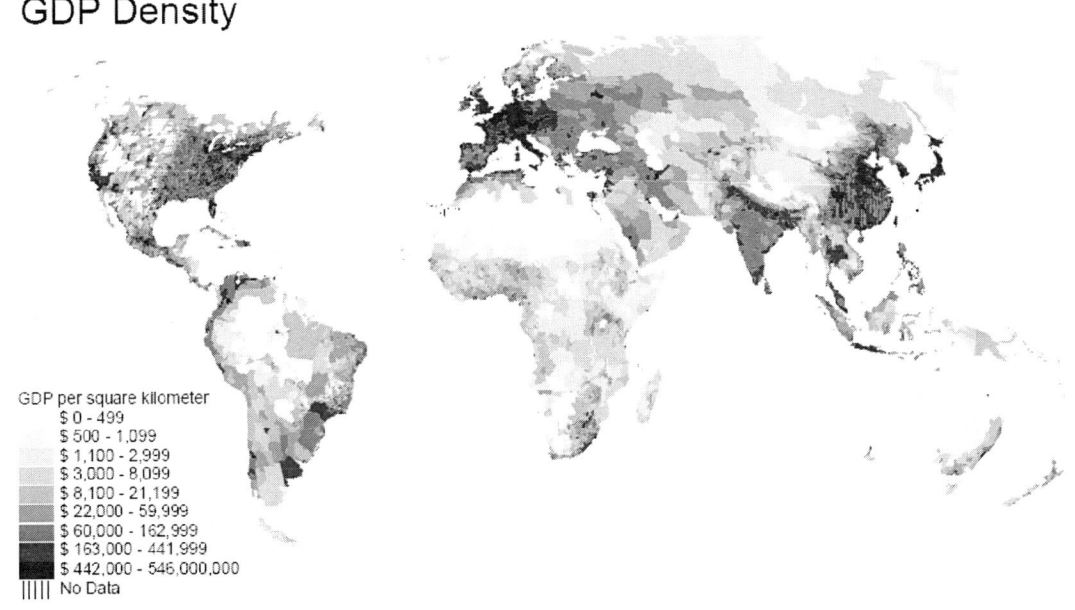

(http://www.econbrowser.com/archives/2007/01/the_distributio.html)

A paper by John Gallup, Jeffrey Sachs and Andrew Mellinger in the International Regional Science Review in 1999 introduced the concept of "GDP density", calculated by multiplying GDP per capita by the number of people per square kilometer. Basically GDP density is a measure of the total amount of economic activity that takes place at different spots on our globe.

Chapter Eleven – Poverty & the Poor

I. Reasons for Poverty

A. Many different factors have been cited to explain why poverty occurs. No single explanation has gained universal acceptance. Factors that have been alleged to cause poverty include:

- State discrimination and corruption. Abuse of public power.
- Lack of social integration. Competition instead of cooperation.
- Crime.
- Substance abuse
- Procrastination
- Natural factors such as climate or environment.
- War, including civil war, genocide, and politicide.
- Lack of education and skills.
- Individual beliefs, actions and choices.

THINKING

Question: What does it mean to be poor? How would YOU define it?

Question: Based on where you live, put a dollar amount ($____.00) on what you would consider the poverty line to be.

Question: If you do not have _____, then you are poor. (just to make a think)

B. Four General Causes of Poverty

(Taken from "Wealth and Poverty" – Kerby Anderson. www.probe.org)

A. __Oppression__ & Fraud (Individuals, Governments)
   Prov 14:31, 22:7, 28:17, James 5:1-4

B. __Misfortune__, __Persecution__, or Judgment
   Job 1:12-19, Psalm 109:16, Lamentations 5:3)

C. __Laziness__, Neglect, Gluttony
   Proverbs 10:4, 13:4, 19:15, 20:13, 23:21)

D. __Culture__ of Poverty
   "Poverty breeds poverty and the cycle is no easily broken" –Kerby Anderson
   Proverbs 10:15 "The ruin of the poor is their poverty."

www.usaid.gov/.../images/photos/surveys-3.jpg

Chapter Eleven – Poverty & the Poor

II. A Biblical View on Wealth & Poverty

(Taken from "Wealth and Poverty" – Kerby Anderson. www.probe.org)

A. Wealth is not Condemned

  Genesis 13:2 (Abraham), Duet 8:28, Prov 22:2

B. When Wealthy People in the Bible were Condemned, it was because of the Means by which the Obtained their Wealth.

  (Amos 4:11, 5:11)

C. Christians should be Concerned about the Effect that Riches can have on our Lives.

  1. We may no longer look to God and even forget Him. (Proverbs 30:8-9, Hosea 13:6)

  2. Pride – (Prov 28:11, Jeremiah 9:2)

III. Biblical Observations on Poverty

A. Poverty _isolates/perpetual_

  Duet 15:11 (Matt 26:11, Mk 14:7, John 12:8)

B. Poverty may be a consequence of sinful personal _choices_. (but not always)

  Proverbs 10:4, 19:15

C. Poverty may be a consequence of sinful choices _made by others_ (but not always)

  James 5:1-4

D. Poverty is not _shameful_

  Jesus was poor – Matt 8:20, 2 Cor 8:9

E. God may have a purpose for the poor – James 2:5

IV. Biblical reasons why Christians should minister to the poor.

A. _God expects it_ – Deut. 15:11; Lev 19:10; I John 3:17

B. Paul's example – Galatians 2:10

C. The principle of sowing and reaping - Galatians 6:7-10; Matthew 5:7

D. God will _reward_ those who give – Proverbs 19:17, 22:9, 28:27

E. When Christians give to the poor they are giving to _Jesus_ - Matthew 25:31-46

Chapter Eleven – Poverty & the Poor

V. A Christian attitude toward the poor

A. Consider others better than ourselves – Philippians 2:3; I Cor 10:24

B. We are not to be a respecter of persons - James 2:1-9

C. We are to love our neighbor as ourselves - Matthew 22:39

D. The Golden Rule - Matthew 7:12; Luke 6:31

E. When you see a need, meet it if you can. - James 4:17' Luke 10 25-37

VI. Ten Principles: giving through an organization

1. **Accountability** – Does the program demand accountability from the people it serves?
2. **Character** – Does the program stress the building of character? "Give a man a fish and feed him for a day. Teach him how to fish and feed him for a lifetime". II Thess 3:10
3. **Discernment** – Do the providers use judgment to give help on an individual basis?
4. **Employment** – Does the program require work of those who can work?
5. **Freedom** – Does the program teach recipients how to free themselves from their dependent status?
6. **God** – Does the program foster true self-esteem by leading them to their creator and His principles?
7. **Success rate** – Does the program have a success rate that can be quantified?
8. **Assessment** – Does the program conduct periodic assessment to determine its effectiveness?
9. **Overhead** – How much money donated goes directly to the poor?
10. **Volunteers** – Are volunteers utilized to keep cost down and to provide a meaningful ministry for people.

Programs that help the poor are intended to be a " _Safety net_ " not a " _Hammock_ ".

VII. Ten suggested activities to make a difference.

1. Volunteer at a soup kitchen
2. Open a food pantry and clothing center in the church
3. Tutor students and adults
4. Provide basic job training
5. Provide child care services for single parents or others who are in real need
6. Be a mentor to children from broken homes
7. Help with Habitat for Humanity
8. Work with urban shelters for the homeless
9. Clean up parks and recreational facilities to provide good activities for kids and families
10. Become informed about the specific needs of your community

www.bluegrassreport.org/.../economy/index.html

Conclusion:

Yes, we feed their bodies but more importantly we must feed them spiritually. Not just bread made by hand, but the Bread of Life (Jesus). Isaiah 61:1 cf; Matt 115

Chapter Eleven – Poverty & the Poor

WORK ETHIC

Chapter Twelve

Applying a Biblical Worldview

Col 3:22-24 (KJV) *Servants, obey in all things [your] masters according to the flesh; not with eyeservice, as menpleasers; but in singleness of heart, fearing God: (23) And whatsoever ye do, do [it] heartily, as to the Lord, and not unto men; (24) Knowing that of the Lord ye shall receive the reward of the inheritance: for ye serve the Lord Christ.*

Col 4: 1 (KJV) *Masters, give unto [your] servants that which is just and equal; knowing that ye also have a Master in heaven.*

Rom 12:11 (NLT) *Never be lazy in your work, but serve the Lord enthusiastically.*

II Thess 3:10-12 (NLT) *Even while we were with you, we gave you this rule: "Whoever does not work should not eat." (11) Yet we hear that some of you are living idle lives, refusing to work and wasting time meddling in other people's business. (12) In the name of the Lord Jesus Christ, we appeal to such people--no, we command them: Settle down and get to work. Earn your own living.*

I. A Biblical Ethic for Work/Business Defined

   A. Work Ethic defined - The applying of moral principles or rules of conduct in business.

work ethic - A set of values based on the moral virtues of hard work and diligence.

_{The American Heritage® Dictionary of the English Language, Fourth Edition copyright ©2000 by Houghton Mifflin Company. Updated in 2009. Published by Houghton Mifflin Company. All rights reserved.}

   B. Christian Worldview (influence)   -   Matt. 5:13-16

(NLT) *13 "You are the salt of the earth. But what good is salt if it has lost its flavor? Can you make it useful again? It will be thrown out and trampled underfoot as worthless. 14 You are the light of the world-like a city on a mountain, glowing in the night for all to see. 15 Don't hide your light under a basket! Instead, put it on a stand and let it shine for all. 16 In the same way, let your good deeds shine out for all to see, so that everyone will praise your heavenly Father.*

      a. Salt- Spiritual influence

      b. Light- Evangelism

II. Principles Related to Business Ethics

A. A Common View of Business Ethics
1. The ultimate purpose of work is to fulfill your self.
2. Success in _life_ means success in work.
3. Success is based on financial _wealth_, professional _recognition_ or _position_.
4. You have got to do _whatever_ it takes to get the job done.

B. A Biblical View of Business Ethics
1. Through work we can love and _serve_ people. Matt. 22:37-40
2. Through work we can meet our own needs and those of our family.
   II Thess. 3:6-12, I Tim. 5:8
3. Through work we can earn money to give to others. Eph. 4:28
4. Through work we can bring _glory to God_. I Cor, 10:31

C. A Biblical View of Work/Money!
1. We are called to work - (Gen 1:28, Ex 20:9, I Thess 4:11)
2. We are not to love the world. - (I John 2:15)
3. We must not be a slave to money. - (Matt 6:24)
4. Money is not the most important priority. - (Mark 6:33, Matt 22:37-40)

D. A Biblical Example! – <u>The Rich Man's Four Big Mistakes</u> (Luke 12:13-21)
- In planning for himself, he forgot his neighbor. (v17)
- In reckoning his goods, he forgot the Giver. (v18)
- In providing for his body (pleasure, treasure, leisure) he forgot his soul. (v19)
- In counting on time (many years) he forgot eternity. (v20)

III. In Relation to my Work Ethic, a Biblical Worldview will affect:

A. How I view work – <u>As a command not a curse.</u>
Six days you shall labor and do all your work – Exodus 20:9.
See also Genesis 1:28; 1 Thessalonians 4:11; Proverbs 6:6-8.

B. How I view my employees – <u>With respect and value.</u>
Masters, be just and fair to your slaves. Remember that you also have a Master—in heaven – Colossians 4:1.   See also James 5:1-6.

C. How I view my employer – <u>With respect and value.</u>
Slaves, obey your earthly masters in everything you do. Try to please them all the time, not just when they are watching you. Serve them sincerely because of your reverent fear of the Lord – Colossians 3:22.   See also 1 Timothy 6:1; 2 Peter 2:18-19.

4. How I approach my work – <u>*As unto the Lord*</u> – Colossians 3:22-23.

5. How I do my work – <u>with honesty and integrity.</u>
Better to be poor and honest than to be dishonest and a fool – Proverbs 19:1.   See also Proverbs 11:1; 18:9; Matthew 5:13-16.

Do what's right, no matter what! How do you view your job? Is the quality of your work affected by the amount of pay you receive?

IV. CSER – and a Biblical Work Ethic.
Applicable to ALL CSER's
A. Be _Considerate_ in your work (attitude)
B. Be on _time_.
C. Be _reliable_.
D. Be _diligent_.
E. Be a good _testimony_ (it reflects on)
  *Christ * Liberty * Your Personal Character

THINKING

1. "It is for us to pray not for tasks equal to our powers, but for powers equal to our tasks, to go forward with a great desire forever beating at the door of our hearts as we travel toward our distant goal." ~ Helen Keller
2. "Success is dependent upon the glands – sweat glands." ~ Zig Ziglar
3. "Big jobs usually go to the men who prove their ability to outgrow small ones." ~ Ralph Waldo Emerson
4. "The average person puts only 25% of his energy and ability into his work." ~ Andrew Carnegie
5. "Talent is never enough. With few exceptions the best players are the hardest workers." ~ Magic Johnson
6. "Things may come to those who wait, but only the things left by those who hustle." ~ Abraham Lincoln

http://www.movemequotes.com/top-25-work-ethic-quotes/

Chapter Twelve – Work Ethic

Chapter Twelve – Work Ethic

CONFLICT RESOLUTION
Applying a Biblical Worldview

Romans 12:18 (KJV) - *If it be possible, as much as lieth in you, live peaceably with all men.*

Matthew 22:37-39 (KJV) - *Thou shalt love the Lord thy God with all thy heart, and with all thy soul, and with all thy mind . This is the first and great commandment. And the second is like unto it, Thou shalt love thy neighbour as thyself.*

Matthew 7:12 (KJV) – The Golden Rule
Therefore all things whatsoever ye would that men should do to you, do ye even so to them.

Life is 10% what happens to you and 90% how you respond!
-Chuck Swindoll

- <u>Right responses</u>
    - relationship building
    - selflessness
    - reconciliation

- <u>Wrong responses</u>
    - anger
    - fight/flight
    - stress
    - frustration

I. Biblical Principles

A. Love <u>God</u>.

Jesus replied, You must love the Lord your God with all your heart, all your soul, and all your mind. This is the first and greatest commandment – Matt 22:37-38. See also 1 Corinthians 10:31.

B. Love <u>others</u>.

And the second is like it: 'Love your neighbor as yourself – Matthew 22:39. See also 1 Corinthians 13:4-8.
  1. Cover in love

    Proverbs 10:12 - *Hatred stirs up strife, but love covers all offenses.*

    Proverbs 19:11 - *Good sense makes one slow to anger, and it is his glory to overlook an offense.*

    1 Peter 4:8 - *Above all, keep loving one another earnestly, since love covers a multitude of sins.*

2. Look into your own heart

   Matthew 7:5 - *You hypocrite, first take the log out of your own eye, and then you will see clearly to take the speck out of your brother's eye.*

   Galatians 6:1 - *Brothers, if anyone is caught in any transgression, you who are spiritual should restore him in a spirit of gentleness. Keep watch on yourself, lest you too be tempted.*

3. Be careful of your <u>words</u>

   Proverbs 15:1 - *A soft answer turns away wrath, but a harsh word stirs up anger.*

   Proverbs 16:21 - *The wise of heart is called discerning, and sweetness of speech increases persuasiveness.*

C. Respect <u>authority</u> - respect the position even when the personality leaves much to be desired.

   Obey your leaders and submit to their authority. They keep watch over you as men who must give an account. Obey them so that their work will be a joy, not a burden, for that would be of no advantage to you – Hebrews 13:17.

D. Apply the Golden Rule.

   So in everything, do to others what you would have them do to you, for this sums up the Law and the Prophets. – Matthew 7:12.

E. Deal with conflict <u>biblically</u> when it does come

   Not every issue has to become a conflict

   Matthew 18:15-17 - *If your brother sins against you, go and tell him his fault, between you and him alone. If he listens to you, you have gained your brother. But if he does not listen, take one or two others along with you, that every charge may be established by the evidence of two or three witnesses. If he refuses to listen to them, tell it to the church. And if he refuses to listen even to the church, let him be to you as a Gentile and a tax collector.*

THINKING

Question: Can "agreeing to disagree" be a legitimate resolution?

Question: Is it possible that a resolution cannot be obtained because one of the parties involved refuses to work through it? Why or why not?

Question: The problem has been resolved… we forgive… but do we forget? What does this mean in how we deal with that individual in the future.

Chapter Thirteen – Conflict Resolution

II. Four Reactions to Conflict

- **"MY WAY"** - I assert my will until you give in. My way is the only way. I'm always right and must always win.
    1. "It's my way or the Highway!"
    2. This person manipulates and refuses to listen.

- **"YOUR WAY"** - I give in. I roll over and play dead. I'm passive and peaceful but also very frustrated.
    1. This is the opposite of the first reaction.
    2. This person is usually unhappy with himself or herself and in the relationship.
    3. Bitterness could eventually ruin this person.

- **"NO WAY"** - I withdraw. I avoid conflict at all costs. I ignore the problem. Nothing is ever resolved.
    1. This person pretends the problem doesn't exist. A sense of self-denial and rationalization is their response.
    2. Anthills can literally become mountains. By the time they are "forced" to respond it is to late.

- **"OUR WAY"** - I care about our relationship and your needs too. So we endeavor to work out mutual goals.
    1. This person is willing to listen and hopes to understand the problem and the person.
    2. Confrontation motivated out of care & love.

III. Assumptions on conflict
A. You have 50% responsibility resolving the conflict.
B. Most conflicts can be resolved and many prevented using the right approach.
C. You can't change people. You can change your own behavior.

IV. Steps in Conflict Resolution

- 1. Define the Problem & Listen
- 2. Show Respect
- 3. Find Solutions
- 4. Reach Agreement
- 5. Follow-Through

1. Listening to discover & define the problem.
    - Do not interrupt while the person is talking
    - Ask questions to understand - Clarify!
    - Restate, paraphrase, summarize facts & feelings
    - Think of the other person's perspective
    - "Seek first to understand, then to be understood" - one of Steven Covey's <u>Seven Habits of Highly Effective People</u>

2. Show Respect to all Participants
    - The point is not who "started it" but how can we "resolve it."
    - Use open body language

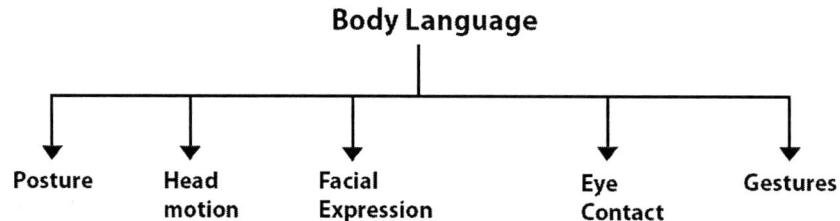

Features of Body Language

- Make eye contact
- Face the speaker
- Show understanding nonverbally - Watch your body language!
- Consider all differences - age, culture, background

Chapter Thirteen – Conflict Resolution

3. Find a Solution

- Seek alternative solutions
- Weigh pros and cons
- Try to find common ground
- Look for common goals, interest, or purpose
- Seek mutual benefits

4. Reach Agreement &   5. Follow Through

- Make sure that <u>you</u> follow the agreement set

PEACEFUL – conflict resolution

- R – respect the right to disagree
- E – express your real concerns
- S – share common goals & interests
- O – open yourself to different points of view
- L – listen carefully to all proposals
- U – understand the major issue involved
- T – think about probable consequences
- I – imagine several alternative solutions
- O – offer reasonable compromises
- N – negotiate mutual cooperative agreement

By Robert E Vallet

Chapter Thirteen – Conflict Resolution

BIBLIOGRAPHY/SUGGESTED READING

Anderson, Kerby. *Christian Ethics in Plain Language*. Nashville: Thomas Nelson, 2005.

Beals, Art. *Beyond Hunger: A Biblical Mandate for Social Responsibility*. Portland, Oregon, Multnomah Press, 1985.

Bonevac, Daniel. *Today's Moral Issues: Classic and Contemporary Perspectives*. New York, New York: McGraw-Hill Companies, 2006.

Boss, Judith A. *Analyzing Moral Issues*. 2nd ed. Boston: McGraw-Hill Companies, 2002.

Boss, Judith A. *Ethics for Life: A Text with Readings*. Boston, McGraw-Hill Companies, 2004.

Clark, David K., and Robert V. Rakestraw. *Readings in Christian Ethics: Issues and Applications*. Vol. 2. Grand Rapids: Baker Books, 2000.

Clark, David K., and Robert V. Rakestraw. *Readings in Christian Ethics: Theory and Method*. Vol. 1. Grand Rapids: Baker Books, 2000.

Colson, Charles., and Nancy Pearcey. *How Shall We Then Live*. Wheaton: Tyndale House Publishers, 1999.

Evan, Tony. *Let's Get To Know Each Other: What White and Black Christians Need to Know About Each Other*. Nashville: Thomas Nelson Publishers, 1995.

Feinberg, John S. and Paul D. *Ethics for a Brave New World*. Wheaton, Illinois: Crossway Books, 2010.

Geisler, Norman L. *Christian Ethics: Contemporary Issues and Options*. Grand Rapids: Baker Books, 2010.

Gibbs, David. *Fighting for Dear Life: The Untold Story of Terri Schiavo and What It Means for All of Us*. Minneapolis, Minnesota: Bethany House, 2006.

Gordon, Wayne L. *Real Hope in Chicago*. Grand Rapids, Michigan: Zondervan Publishing House, 1995.

Green, Joel B., gen. ed. *Dictionary of Scripture and Ethics*. Grand Rapids, Michigan: Baker Academic, 2011.

Grudem, Wayne. *Business for the Glory of God: The Bible's Teaching on the Moral Goodness of Business*. Wheaton, Illinois: Crossway, 2003.

_____. *Countering the Claims of Evangelical Feminism: Biblical Responses to the Key Questions*. Colorado Springs, Colorado: Multnomah Publishers, 2006.

_____. *Politics According to the Bible: A Comprehensive Resource for Understanding Modern Political Issues in Light of Scripture.* Grand Rapids, Michigan: Zondervan, 2010.

Harris, Joshua. *I Kissed Dating Goodbye.* Sisters, Oregon: Multnomah Books, 1997.

Heimbach, Daniel R. *True Sexual Morality: Recovering Biblical Standards for a Culture in Crisis.* Wheaton, Illinois: Crossway Books, 2004.

Hogsett, Jim A. *A Worker Need Not Be Ashamed: How to Live the Christian Life in the Workplace.* 1st Books, 2004.

Hollinger, Dennis. *Choosing the Good: Christian Ethics in a Complex World.* Grand Rapids, Michigan: Baker Academic, 2002.

_____. *The Meaning of Sex: Christian Ethics and the Moral Life.* Grand Rapids, Michigan: Baker Academic, 2009.

Humphrey, Derek. *Dying with Dignity: Understanding Euthanasia.* New York: Carol Publishing Group, 1992.

Kilner John F. *Why The Church Needs Bioethics: A Guide to Wise Engagement with Life's Challenges.* Grand Rapids, Michigan: Zondervan, 2011.

Kostenberger, Andreas J. *God, Marriage, and Family: Rebuilding the Biblical Foundation.* Wheaton, Illinois: Crossway Books, 2004.

Lapin, Daniel. *America's Real War.* Sisters, Oregon: Multnomah Publishers, 1999.

Levine, Carol. *Taking Sides: Clashing Views on Bioethical Issues.* Dubuque, Iowa: McGraw-Hill Company, 2008.

Murray, John. *Principles of Conduct: Aspects of Biblical Ethics.* Grand Rapids, Michigan: William B. Eerdmans Publishing Company, 1957.

Pearcey, Nancy. *Total Truth: Liberating Christianity from Its Cultural Captivity.* Wheaton, Illinois: Crossway Books, 2004.

Piper, John. *Bloodlines: Race, Cross, and the Christian.* Wheaton, Illinois: Crossway, 2011.

Piper, John and Wayne Grudem, ed. *Recovering Biblical Manhood and Womanhood: A Response to Evangelical Feminism.* Wheaton, Illinois: Crossway Books, 1991, 2006.

Rae, Scott B. *Moral Choices: An Introduction to Ethics.* Grand Rapids, Michigan: Zondervan, 2009.

Satris, Stephen. *Taking Sides: Clashing Views on Moral Issues.* Dubuque, Iowa: McGraw-Hill Company, 2008.

Shapiro, Ben. *Brainwashed: How Universities Indoctrinate America's Youth*. Nashville: WND Books, 2004.

Swindoll, Charles R. *Sanctity of Life The Inescapable Issue*. Dallas: Word Publishing, 1990.

Talley, Jim A. and Bobbie Reed. *Too Close Too Soon: Avoiding the Heartache of Premature Intimacy*. Nashville: Thomas Nelson Publishers, 2002.

VanDrunen, David. *Bioethics and the Christian Life: A Guide to Making Difficult Decisions*. Wheaton, Illinois: Crossway, 2009.

Wilkens, Steve. *Beyond Bumper Sticker Ethics*. Downers Grove: Intervarsity Press, 1995.

Williams, Jarvis J. *One New Man: The Cross and Racial Reconciliation in Pauline Theology*. Nashville, Tennessee: B&H Academic, 2010.